ROYAL STYLE

LE CONCERT CHAMPÊTRE *by Giorgione: one of the most celebrated masterpieces*
from the collection of Charles I. When Charles's collections were dispersed by Cromwell,
this picture was snapped up for the French royal collections.
Important paintings have always been one of the most desirable
status symbols for monarchs to acquire

ROYAL STYLE

FIVE CENTURIES OF INFLUENCE AND FASHION

STEPHEN CALLOWAY AND STEPHEN JONES

LITTLE BROWN AND COMPANY

BOSTON · TORONTO · LONDON

First U.S. Edition

First published in Great Britain 1991 by Pyramid Books

ISBN 0 316 12509 1

Library of Congress Catalog Card Number 91-52938

Library of Congress Cataloging-in-Publication information is available

10 9 8 7 6 5 4 3 2 1

Printed in Hong Kong

Editor: Anne Crane
Art Editor: Robin Whitecross
Picture Researcher: Julia Pashley

CONTENTS

PROLOGUE   6

THE AGE OF PAGEANTRY 15
16   Maximilian I
22   Henry VIII
28   François I
34   Elizabeth I
40   Cosimo I de' Medici
46   Philip II

THE AGE OF GRANDEUR 53
54   Rudolf II
60   Marie de' Medici and Louis XIII
66   Charles I
72   Christina of Sweden
78   Louis XIV
84   Charles II

THE AGE OF TASTE   91
92   Augustus the Strong
98   Louis XV
104   Frederick the Great
110   Catherine the Great
116   Gustav III
122   Louis XVI and Marie Antoinette

THE AGE OF OPULENCE   129
130   Napoleon I
136   George IV
142   Victoria and Albert
148   Napoleon III and Eugénie
154   Ludwig II
160   Nicholas and Alexandra

THE AGE OF DEMOCRACY 167
168   Edward VII
174   Marie of Romania
180   Queen Mary
186   Edward VIII
192   Queen Elizabeth the Queen Mother
198   The Prince and Princess of Wales

BIBLIOGRAPHY   204

INDEX   204

ACKNOWLEDGEMENTS   208

Renaissance pageantry reached new imaginative heights
in the sequence of extraordinary woodcuts created at the beginning
of the sixteenth century under the direction of Hans Burgkmair
for the glorification of the Emperor Maximilian

PROLOGUE

Our theme is ostentation, for throughout history conspicuous display has been an essential component in the trappings of monarchy. Medieval kings and queens had, of course, employed pageantry as a form of propaganda both in war and peace. The language of heraldry had been vital to the survival of military rulers and their knights on the field of battle and its identifying symbols upon helm and shield became the basis of all courtly panoply. But this display was rooted in the grim realities of ferocious warlords and unstable governments.

Treasuries and treasures were the prerogative of the church and it was the spiritual princes of the Middle Ages who first made the equation between temporal power and artistic glory. For in the monasteries and cathedral churches of Europe craftsmen laboured to create glittering chalices, crucifixes and reliquaries, all of which, though dedicated to the greater glory of God, stated unequivocally the wealth and might of the Church. Envious princes often coveted the lustre which ownership of such rare objects bestowed upon their overweening prelates. But the combination of faith and superstition which governed the medieval mind preserved the power of the Church.

The dawn of the Renaissance brought a new secularism, fuelled by the rediscovery of pagan antiquity. Scholars, freed from the dry dogmas of religious studies, redefined the world, making man the measure of all things. Throughout Europe princes were set to study Greek and Roman texts and derived from their tutors a model of kingship based upon the noblest ancient precedents. As these young men of the fifteenth century grew to maturity and entered upon their inheritances they brought to their courts a new and gracious civilisation. It is here that our story begins.

The cultural attainments of François I or Henry VIII are but part of a princely ideal to which such men aspired. Their world was not limited to the bleak *Realpolitik* recommended by that cynical political theorist, Niccolò Machiavelli. They aspired not merely to be rulers but to embrace all the attainments of the Renaissance Man. In this they followed the template of the noble prince as scholar, patron and philosopher, as defined by Baldassare Castiglione in his treatise

OVERLEAF: This panorama of the EMBARKATION OF HENRY VIII, by an unknown artist, conveys well the drama of court life. Soldiers, sailors and courtiers are all caught up in the tremendous panoply of a royal occasion

ABOVE: *Ludwig II of Bavaria, who aspired to emulate the autocratic rule of his hero Louis XIV, was an isolated and alienated figure in democratic nineteenth-century Europe.* OPPOSITE: *Versailles, the monumental palace complex, which grew more like a miniature royal city under the reign of Louis XIV. The king, fearful of the power of the aristocracy in their own provinces, forced his courtiers to dance attendance upon him at every hour of the day*

*Above Left: Tsar Nicholas II of Russia and his family. He was the last monarch who sought
to impose absolute rule upon his people. Above Right: Princess Louisa and Prince James, of the house of Stuart.
Acquired by Queen Elizabeth the Queen Mother, it is typical of the associative collecting which the members
of the house of Windsor have cultivated in this century. Opposite: Edward VIII, as Duke of Windsor, commissioned
this bejewelled flamingo brooch as a gift for Wallis Simpson, the woman for whom he gave up his throne.
It is typical of his generosity in showering her with the smart modern jewellery she craved*

The Book of the Courtier. Royal patronage was seen as the ideal vehicle by which to demonstrate both a profound love of all the arts and the power to command.

Royal collecting became a European obsession, for the pursuit of rare objects advertised not only the taste but, equally importantly, the wealth of the patron. When Charles I bought from the rulers of Mantua their great picture collection, many perceived the house of Stuart to have been greatly aggrandized by this transaction, whilst no less surely that of Gonzaga was demeaned. At the pinnacle of his power Charles possessed the finest collection of paintings ever assembled. When Cromwell sold them off, these masterpieces became the prizes of many of the great European collections, celebrated not only for their beauty but for their distinguished provenance.

By the eighteenth century royal collecting was carried out on a vast scale. Palaces were built to accommodate ever-growing collections, whilst the creation of this architecture itself generated an almost insatiable demand for sumptuous decoration and furnishings. Louis XIV had established a bench mark for magnificence, making

Versailles the symbol of his power and the envy of Europe. Imitation being, as it is said, the sincerest form of flattery, the lesser monarchs of the period strove to emulate in some degree the splendours of the Sun King.

The drama of European monarchy was in the nineteenth century acted out against an impossibly romantic backdrop of castles and palaces built to evoke the splendours of past ages. The most extraordinary of these were the stage-set fantasies contrived by mad King Ludwig of Bavaria from his operatic dreams of Wagnerian legend. In a strange way the homely baronial Gothic favoured by Victoria and Albert at Balmoral is just as much a piece of play acting, though here the scene is one which celebrates domesticity, rather than one cast in Ludwig's sublime vein of comic tragedy.

Real tragedy struck in the twentieth century with the fateful pistol-shot at Sarajevo, which echoed throughout Europe as crowns and eagles fell. The collapse of the imperial regime in Russia and the murder of the tsar and his family brought home to other reigning monarchs the need to redefine their role and cultivate a new royal style, founded upon an acceptance of the democratic principle and marked by a subtle reticence. Today European monarchy aims to maintain its rich heritage of patronage, but the taste and collecting of modern rulers has become characterised by gracious informality and a concern for the well-being of their people.

16TH CENTURY

THE AGE OF PAGEANTRY

'There's such divinity doth hedge a King....'
Shakespeare: HAMLET, Act iv, Scene 5

MAXIMILIAN I

Few monarchs have done as much in their own lifetimes to ensure that their memory would be enshrined in splendour of word and image as the Emperor Maximilian. Yet by a curious paradox he achieved very little. Even the glorious self-image of the emperor as a latter-day Charlemagne lacks any real historical substance and is largely the product of carefully orchestrated artistic propaganda.

The Germany of which Maximilian became king in 1486 was a loosely allied federation of small principalities, independent bishoprics and free cities, whose princes, bishops and burghers retained a fiercely proud sense of their autonomy. Individual rivalries were set aside only when these petty potentates were obliged, as Electors, to come together to select a new Holy Roman Emperor. In 1493 they chose Maximilian, thus placing upon his shoulders the dual responsibility of promoting the interests of the German lands while defending those of the sprawling Empire.

Maximilian's life was spent constantly moving from one part of his dominions to another, protecting his subjects in one place only to find that in another part of his realm revolution was imminent. At one time, in 1488, he was even imprisoned by the people of Bruges, held in his own city until he had answered their complaints. The image of Maximilian as knight errant, incessantly in pursuit of chivalric glory, accords well with his temperament, for in many respects he was as much a figure from the late medieval world as a prince of the Renaissance, called by his wondering contemporaries 'the last of the knights'.

Maximilian wished to ensure two things: the dynastic security of his own Hapsburg family and an immortal place for himself amongst the heroes of chivalric legend. The first of these objectives required prodigious expenditure on mercenary armies and their extended campaigns. This so drained Maximilian's coffers that he was obliged time and again to go cap in hand to the diplomats and bankers of Europe in search of funds. Even Henry VIII considered him a bad financial risk, whilst to the suspicious Florentine bankers he was known as Maximilian of the Empty Purse.

One result of this was that Maximilian's activities as a patron of the arts, although enthusiastic, tended

Albrecht Dürer's subtle and masterly drawing of Maximilian I conveys the artist's clear understanding of his master's character. Dürer's angular draughtsmanship, like Maximilian's imagination, is steeped in the world of the Middle Ages. But, noble and wilful, chivalric and cunning, Maximilian looks out upon a world in a ferment of change

to be sporadic. His greatest undertaking and indeed his lifelong preoccupation was to be the creation of a vast iconographic tomb, cast in bronze for the Hofkirche in his capital at Innsbruck. He began to plan this *Grabmal* as early as 1502, consulting scholars, artists and craftsmen on the symbolic and technical problems of creating a vast gallery of 40 life-size figures including portraits of his real and legendary ancestors. Prominent amongst the figures were to be the Nine Worthies, heroes of medieval and early Renaissance literature, including King Arthur of Britain, the very model of royal knighthood. Of the eleven statues completed within Maximilian's lifetime, those of Arthur and Theodoric the Ostrogoth, wrought by Peter Vischer of Nuremberg, are certainly the finest. Though the designs for at least two other figures were made by Albrecht Dürer, a number of craftsmen of varying degrees of skill were involved over a period of years and the tomb, with a final complement of 28 figures, was at last completed in 1566 by Maximilian's grandson, Ferdinand.

The emperor was fortunate, in his search for artists and craftsmen, that the fine and decorative arts were in a flourishing state in the German lands at the turn of the fifteenth century. Albeit for the most part untouched by

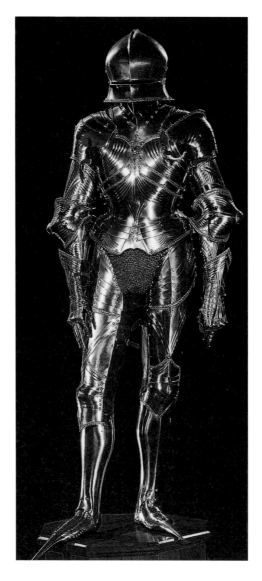

Italianate ideas, this native tradition was rich in ingenious ornament and curious imagination. Foremost among the artists working for Maximilian on the *Grabmal* and his many other projects was of course Dürer, who had travelled in Italy, where his reputation, in particular with the leading artists of Venice especially stood high.

Maximilian's patronage of Dürer

was coloured by his warm personal regard for the artist. He was very direct and easy in his dealings with all kinds of people, and did not stand upon his dignity as a king and emperor. In particular he enjoyed watching Dürer and other artists at work. One of the many stories associated with Maximilian tells how, while watching Dürer working on a mural, the emperor asked one of his courtiers to hold the ladder on which the artist stood. This noble in turn told his servant to steady the steps, considering it too menial a task for him to undertake Maximilian reprimanded him for his arrogance, pointing out that he as emperor could make any peasant into a nobleman, but that no nobleman could aspire to Dürer's artistic genius.

Maximilian employed Dürer to draw exquisite images in the margins of a prayer book designed for his personal use. In this he once more looked back to the Middle Ages, to the older tradition of illuminated manuscripts. However, he was also the first monarch to explore fully the potential of the new technology of letterpress printing, by commissioning from a number of expert woodcut artists a sequence of grandiose portraits to be issued widely as single-sheet prints. In this way his image was carried to all parts of the Empire. Another project, intended perhaps to hand down to

ABOVE: This detail of the reliefs on the tomb of Maximilian in the Hofkirche in Innsbruck reveals the magnificent quality of the carving which the emperor commissioned. OPPOSITE: Maximilian's armour was of the finest quality obtainable in Europe. By this date armourers, especially those in the imperial workshops at Augsburg, had raised their craft to its artistic peak

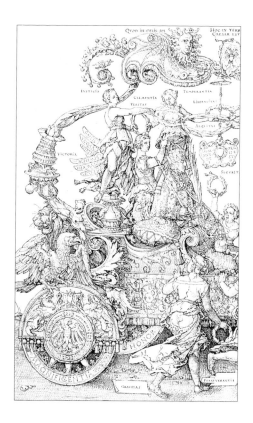

*ABOVE: Maximilian's own vision of himself as triumphant Holy Roman
Emperor was bolstered by grandiose fantasies such as the great series of woodcuts
by Hans Burgkmair, known as THE TRIUMPH OF MAXIMILIAN.
OPPOSITE: This portrait of Maximilian surrounded by his family strikes a warmer
and more personal note, showing the emperor in a rare moment of domestic
calm. It is the work of his court painter, Bernhard Strigel*

posterity an image of the emperor's achievements, was a series of magnificently illustrated books containing fictionalised accounts of his life as a soldier, hunter and romantic hero. The idea for these seems to have grown out of the *Jagdbuch* and *Fischereibuch*, two hand-drawn albums of coloured illustrations of the imperial hunting and fishing grounds. The three most significant books are the *Teurdank, Freydal* and *Weisskonig* in which over 600 woodcuts convey a vivid if somewhat imaginary picture of the emperor's glorious deeds.

Perhaps the most remarkable products of this programme of graphic aggrandisement are the two large set pieces, *The Triumph of Maximilian* masterminded by the talented woodcut artist Hans Burgkmair, and the unique *Triumphal Arch*, created under Dürer's direction: a vast paper monument to insubstantial ambition.

SI IVVAT HEROVM CLARAS VIDISSE FIGVRAS,
SPECTA HAS, MAIORES NVLLA TABELLA TVLIT.
CERTAMEN MAGNVM, LIS, QVESTIO MAGNA PATERNE
FILIVS AN VINCAT, VICIT VTERQVE QVIDEM.
ISTE SVOS HOSTES PATRIÆQVE INCENDIA SÆPE
SVSTVLIT, ET PACEM CIVIBVS VSQVE DEDIT.

FILIVS AD MAIORA QVIDEM PROGNATVS AB ARIS
SVBMOVET INDIGNOS SVBSTITVITQVE PROBOS.
CERTÆ VIRTVTI PAPARVM AVDACIA CESSIT,
HENRICO OCTAVO SCEPTRA GERENTE MANV
REDDITA RELIGIO EST, ISTO REGNANTE DEIQVE
DOGMATA CEPERVNT ESSE IN HONORE SVO.

PROTOTYPVM IVSTÆ MAGNITVDINIS IPSO OPERE TECTORIO
FECIT HOLBENIVS IVBENTE HENRICO VIII.
ECTYPVM A REMIGIO VAN LEEMPVT BREVIORI TABELLA
DESCRIBI VOLVIT CAROLVS II. M. B. F. & H. R.
Aº. D. M. MDCLXVII.

HENRY VIII

The shrewd political sense of the founder of the Tudor dynasty, Henry VII, had enabled him to establish his family as rulers of a stable kingdom. His son Henry VIII had no need to be a warrior king within his own realm. Looking beyond the English Channel to where strife both secular and religious was reshaping the map of Europe, he recognised the vital importance of successful propaganda to his continuing power. The young king assumed the style and status of a great Renaissance ruler in a spirit of friendly yet serious rivalry with François I of France and the Emperor Maximilian.

Henry's first great artistic commission was at once an act of family piety and an enlightened recognition of the importance of the new artistic ideas then coming out of Italy. He brought to England the Florentine sculptor Pietro Torrigiano to create a bronze tomb which would enshrine the old king amongst the bones of his legitimate predecessors in Westminster Abbey. Thus in the midst of the medieval royal necropolis was set the first great classical work of art on English soil.

Henry's awareness of the international scene brought to his court not only diplomats but also artists and designers. Among these was the brilliant draughtsman Hans Holbein. His portrait miniature of Anne of Cleves was an all-too-flattering likeness, for it convinced Henry to make the plain 'Flanders mare' his fourth queen. But in spite of that Holbein established himself in an unassailable position as the royal image-maker. He painted not only the definitive likeness of the king by which all others have been judged, but also a great mural at Whitehall Palace celebrating the establishment and vitality of the Tudors.

It was not, however, enough for a Renaissance prince to exhibit his cultivation merely by tossing commissions to artists as others might bones to a dog. In the age of Erasmus and Thomas More a king had to be able to do more than merely write his name: he had to display some real learning if he was to hold his own with the more intellectual of his servants and courtiers. Henry's accomplishments were probably well above the average. He was adept at writing love poems and composed a number of popular tunes, amongst which *Greensleeves* has

The might and majesty of the early Tudor dynasty was exemplified in Hans Holbein's Whitehall mural decoration which survives only in a copy by Remegius van Leemput. Henry VII and Elizabeth of York look down upon their son, Henry VIII and his wife of the moment, Jane Seymour. OVERLEAF: THE FIELD OF THE CLOTH OF GOLD, by Johannes Corvus, records the most sumptuous diplomatic encounter of the age

*The gatehouse of Hampton Court, the great brick palace built by
Cardinal Wolsey and appropriated by his envious master*

remained one of the most enduring of all English melodies.

In 1521 he published a celebrated tract denouncing Martin Luther, the German monk whose heretical writings precipitated the Reformation. This intelligent piece of propaganda won Henry the gratitude of the pope, who granted to the Crown of England the title Defender of the Faith. That Henry proudly displayed this title on his coinage and elsewhere proved ultimately to be the greatest of ironies. Within a decade the pope's champion had become his bitterest foe. Henry's battle to overthrow the power of the Catholic Church in England was a stormy one. He brought to bear the full force of his propaganda machine, declaring himself supreme head of a new Church of England and sparking off a great wave of antipapal feeling. *The Four Evangelists stoning the Pope*, a violent painting by Giralamo de Treviso, commissioned by Henry, gave potent visual form to the king's rage against the papacy.

Henry was as passionate in love as he was in his anger. In the course of his life he wooed many women and his greatest claim to popular historical fame rests on the six marriages he made. Indeed, in every area of sensuous delight his appetites were voracious; but he was by nature a fickle lover, not only of women, but also of horses, hunting dogs and architecture.

He inherited a palace at Whitehall which remained the centre of his administration and urban court life.

Holbein was much employed there, turning his hand to projects such as the design of the great gatehouse, which bore his name. All the other residences for which Henry really cared were more in the nature of pleasure pavilions. The king loved to ride out from his palace at Greenwich to the simpler hunting lodge at Eltham. But of all the many houses and castles which he owned Nonesuch was his favourite, and expressed most fully the curious and often delightful manner in which the ornaments of the classical style were grafted piecemeal on to the old vernacular building traditions. Foreign craftsmen were brought to work alongside English builders, creating strange hybrid forms. Outside, the palace presented a

Helmet for ceremonial parades, in the form of a grotesque, horned head, made by the imperial armourers of Augsburg and sent as a diplomatic gift by Maximilian to Henry VIII

vast frontage, flanked by stout corner turrets but topped with a fantastical skyline composed of statues and urns in the latest Italianate taste. Within, the palace's great halls were similarly eclectic: hangings of rich Flemish tapestry contrasted with the brilliant whiteness or sometimes strong colours of novel stucco chimneypieces.

Richness, splendour and display were the keynotes of the court of Henry VIII. Ostentatious opulence was as much the prerogative of the peacock male courtier as of the female. Henry's broad frame made him the greatest clotheshorse of his age, whether costumed for a court revel in silks and jewels or buckled into his magnificent armour for a mock battle. Though Henry never fought a real war, much less led troops in the field, the panoply of war played a major part in the image of his kingship. At Deptford the royal shipyards built some of the greatest warships of the age, towering galleons like the *Ark Royal* and the ill-fated *Mary Rose*. The great love of armour, which Henry shared with the Emperor Maximilian, led him to establish workshops at Greenwich where magnificent pieces of parade armour and weapons were made for the royal jousts. Spectacular tournaments between mounted knights were at one level a hangover from the Middle Ages: but Henry cleverly used these stylized chivalric conflicts as a showcase of national might, making them a vital component in the summit conferences of the age. The greatest of these occasions was undoubtedly the Field of the Cloth of Gold, upon which Henry and his royal cousin François I strutted like proud turkeycocks.

FRANÇOIS I

When Robert de la Marck, a daring soldier of fortune, recalled the youth of his master, François I, he was struck by the high spirits and precocious learning of the future king. 'I think', he wrote, 'no Prince ever had more pastimes than my said lord, or was better instructed, by the provision of my lady his mother.'

At the castle of Amboise, where François grew up, tennis and jousting alternated with the study of Latin and the old histories of France. The chivalric romances, especially the *Life of Charlemagne*, which delighted the young men of François's circle, celebrated in word and picture the glorious martial traditions of France. Even before he became king in 1515 François had tasted battle in military campaigns, in particular against the English forces of his lifelong rival, Henry VIII. At the same time he had begun to develop that passion for the courtly graces which was to make him in the eyes of his contemporaries the very model of a king, epitomising that 'handsomeness of person and beauty of visage ... great majesty' and 'a certain lovely courtesy' which were set up as an ideal by the great Italian writer Baldassare Castiglione in his manual of Renaissance princedom, *The Book of the Courtier*.

All men looked to Italy for standards of taste and scholarship in this age, but François looked south not only as a connoisseur but also as a soldier king seeking to extend his sphere of influence. In 1516, little more than a year after succeeding to the throne, he descended upon northern Italy, where he defeated the troops of the Holy Roman Empire at the Battle of Marignano and entered Milan in triumph. Pope Leo X met the French king at Bologna and confirmed this victory by forging a diplomatic alliance with him. This historic realignment of political forces was recorded and celebrated that same year: Raphael, then at work in the papal apartments at the Vatican on a great mural of the coronation of Charlemagne, gave to the principal figures of the emperor and the pope the features of François and Leo X.

In Milan François was astonished by Leonardo da Vinci's recently completed painting of *The Last Supper*, but even the all-conquering hero was unable to acquire a picture which was

The portrait of a handsome sensualist: Jean Clouet's likeness
of François I reflects that monarch's grace, charm and fashionable hauteur.
His costume, replete with heavily padded velvets and brocades,
seems intended to add weight to the king's dignity

*ABOVE: Benvenuto Cellini's great gold and enamel saltcellar,
made for François I, is undoubtedly the most remarkable achievement of the
goldsmith's craft in the High Renaissance period.
OPPOSITE: THE VIRGIN OF THE ROCKS, one of the celebrated paintings
acquired by François l directly from Leonardo da Vinci*

A detail from a fresco in the long gallery at Fontainebleau which was decorated by the great Italian Mannerist, Francesco Primaticcio. It records the appearance of the château at the time of François I, when it was the dynamic focus of a whole new school of art, which had been brought into being by the king's patronage

painted in fresco on a wall. Instead, he decided to acquire the painter, and the ageing Leonardo agreed to undertake the journey to France and settle at François's court as the most honoured of the many foreign artists and craftsmen drawn to the north by the artistic ambition of the young king.

François spent lavishly to establish his status as a great collector and in a very short time he had brought together the finest collection of pictures north of the Alps. Though Leonardo failed, in the three years before he died at Amboise, to complete any major work for his new patron, he did bring with him three of his masterpieces: the *Mona Lisa*, the *Virgin of the Rocks* and the *St John the Baptist*. François's enthusiasm for the work and the company of living artists led him to issue invitations to many of the greatest of the day. Michelangelo declined, and François had to content himself with the acquisition of a small *Hercules* from the hand of the most celebrated sculptor of the age. Many others, however, did enter the royal service, including the Florentine artist Andrea del Sarto, whose great *Madonna* had caught the eye of his discerning new patron.

All François's tastes in art and architecture were founded upon his experiences in Italy and he had even sat to Titian, so it is ironic that the greatest portrait of the king is from the hand of a Fleming, Jean Clouet, who rose by the 1520s to be his court painter. Clouet's hard, northern, enamelled style precisely captures the splendour and arrogance of the prince who rode out of Calais to meet Henry VIII at the Field of the Cloth of Gold. This magnificent piece of courtly ceremonial united the already old-fashioned chivalric codes of the two kings' youth with the new imperatives of European diplomacy.

François was a modern monarch and at Blois and Chambord he took the ancient royal fortresses and transformed them into glittering Renaissance palaces. The latest ideas of the Italian architects Bramante and Domenico da Cortona were grafted on to the native tradition of fanciful ornament. However, the costly wars and humiliating defeats of the 1520s diverted François from major building projects until, chastened by his defeat at Pavia in 1525 and subsequent year-long imprisonment in Spain, he sought peace and renewal in the creation of the grandest of hunting lodges, at Fontainebleau in the great boar forests to the south of Paris.

The team of architects and craftsmen that François assembled to work on the new château has become known as the School of Fontainebleau. Its prime leaders were the artists Rosso Fiorentino and Francesco Primaticcio, who together with a number of French designers elaborated a highly distinctive version of the then current Italian Mannerist style. To this palace François brought many of his greatest treasures, including pictures, the royal library, and many of the casts of antique statues that his agents had secured in Italy. New pictures in the Mannerist style were particularly sought after and foreign heads of state, knowing that such gifts would find favour, sent the best of their artists' work; from Cosimo de' Medici came the bizarre but fascinating allegory *Venus and Cupid with Time* by Agnolo Bronzino.

In 1540 there arrived at Fontainebleau the colourful figure of the goldsmith Benvenuto Cellini, full of artistic ingenuity. François was eager to employ Cellini but like many other patrons found it difficult to make him finish any one project. The exception was a great golden saltcellar, a masterpiece of the Italian's workmanship which was recognised as a wonder of the age. Such works ensured that, on his death in 1547, François was mourned, not as an Alexander, but as a Maecenas.

ELIZABETH I

When Queen Elizabeth's father, Henry VIII, established in England a new dissident church, he unleashed religious controversy and civil strife which tore asunder the fabric of English society for two generations. After the unhappy reign of her Catholic half-sister, Mary, Elizabeth brought to the throne an ideal of strong Protestant government. Having herself lived in fear of death for her religious persuasion, she was determined, by allowing a degree of religious toleration, to secure stability and thereby prosperity.

However, the widespread unrest which crippled continental Europe in the middle years of the century made Elizabeth's task very difficult. Not only was she a Protestant monarch at bay, she was also uniquely and astonishingly an unsupported woman holding political sway without the hand of a male consort to guide her. This was at once her weakness and her strength, for it allowed her to play off favourites and allies one against another, but finally to rely upon none of them. Her isolation was her glory: and she reigned as Gloriana, casting herself in the role of the Virgin Queen.

This role, dramatised by poets and realised by artists, wove together numerous strands of chivalric tradition, ancient British history and classical mythology. These elements together formed a rich background to the powerful and glamorous figure that the queen presented to her contemporaries. As a young woman her fair complexion and golden hair accorded perfectly with the image. She chose with care both her clothes and accessories, so that, garbed in white or silver and encrusted with jewels, she appeared to her court, and to portraitists to whom she deigned to grant a sitting, an image as dazzling as a Catholic statue of the Madonna.

Always highly conscious of the effect of paintings and printed portraits as propaganda, Elizabeth as the years progressed deliberately froze her image into her so-called 'Mask of Beauty'. This was not merely the result of vanity, but revealed a shrewd perception of her need, in the political arena, to appear aloof yet desirable and still potentially the mother of an heir. Her chosen painter was Nicholas Hilliard, whose decorative miniatures and noble half-length paintings showed the royal face pale, unshad-

A curious symbolic portrait of Queen Elizabeth I by Hans Eworth, in which
the queen is depicted in the act of claiming for herself the golden orb, symbolising England,
rather than awarding it to any one of the three goddesses, Juno, Minerva or Venus
who feature in the legend of the Judgement of Paris

ABOVE: In this illustration from a manuscript, the queen is shown receiving a volume from the hand of the poet George Gascoigne. She is seated in one of the so-called 'sea-dog' chairs, long held to be emblematic of English sea power. OPPOSITE: The Armada Jewel, one of several precious lockets containing miniature portraits of Elizabeth by Nicholas Hilliard, given by the queen to her loyal subjects

owed and unchanging. Other artists conformed to this pattern, while presenting the queen in a variety of symbolic roles. She was Diana, the chaste huntress, the Faerie Queen of Spenser's poem, and, in a picture by Hans Eworth that is the most curious of all these images, she puts to rout all other goddesses from the field, claiming for herself the golden apple that is the orb of England.

Spectacle played a major part in Elizabethan court life. Lavish ceremonies and intricately staged masques were a huge drain on the royal finances, whilst by contrast the queen's annual progresses around the country brought all this splendour to the provinces at the expense of those loyal but unfortunate courtiers upon whose houses she descended. Each year, too, Elizabeth presided over a remarkable piece of theatrical pageantry called the Accession Day Tilt, in which her knights paraded in a chivalric celebration of their loyalty to the Tudor dynasty.

Though she clearly revelled in this ritualised pugnacity among her favourites and tacitly encouraged the daring of her sea captains as licensed pirates, the guiding principle of the queen's foreign policy was always to avoid open war, while promoting and safeguarding trade. The great navy built up by her father was supplemented now by armed merchant ships which ventured in search of legitimate trade and Spanish plunder. Commerce was vital to England and the new generation of middle-class Protestant entrepreneurs served their queen well, acting very often as informal ambassadors in far-flung courts such as that of Ivan the Terrible, Tsar of all the Russias.

Sir Francis Drake was notable among the merchant venturers who served the queen, for his exploits against the Spanish, having 'singed the King of Spain's beard' by burning the fleet in the harbour at Cadiz. He won wealth and honours from his monarch for sailing around the world and returning with his ship, the *Golden Hind*, laden with gold and jewels from the New World.

However great that triumph, Drake remains best remembered for his role in the defeat of the Spanish Armada in 1588. That this piece of English folklore has proved so enduring is a tribute to the power of the Elizabethan propaganda machine. The legend of the dispersal of a mighty fleet of pompous galleons by a tiny band of wily sea dogs was invented by the queen and her ministers and has for ever clouded the truth. The weather rather than her sea power saved England, sinking or wrecking the greater number of the Spanish ships.

England's great victory was celebrated in a profusion of paintings, popular prints and medals. The most associative of these mementos is the Drake Jewel, wrought by an unknown goldsmith and containing a portrait of the queen by Hilliard. This exquisite object was given by the grateful queen to England's trustiest sailor, who, in the fashion of royal favourites, is seen wearing it in several portraits. For Drake it was an honour for a dangerous but successful enterprise, but for Elizabeth it was yet one more shrewd and unsentimental recognition of the value of princely munificence.

Etiquette at court ensured that the queen was the prime female focus of all attention. This painting of Elizabeth being carried in procession by her courtiers conveys well the manner in which she dominated all ceremonial entertainment and formal pageantry. The noblemen gather like moths around a flame, in search of favour and preferment

COSIMO I DE' MEDICI

The great mercantile city of Florence had in the fifteenth century been fiercely proud of its status as a republic. Bowing to neither princes nor prelates, Florentines nonetheless looked for leadership to one family, the great international bankers and patrons of the arts, the Medici. The pride and ever-growing power of the family caused them to be expelled from the city on more than one occasion, but each time they returned it was with greater strength.

Even within the family there was continual jockeying for political power. In 1537 Lorenzino de' Medici, seeing himself as a second Brutus, assasinated his cousin, Alessandro, whose overweening rule, like that of Julius Caesar, smacked of incipient despotism. The 18-year-old Cosimo, descendant of a minor branch of the family, was thrust on to the ducal throne. However, far from being the mere pawn of his power-hungry family, Cosimo resolutely embarked upon the course that would establish his absolute rule.

The first step in his power-broking was to make a sound political marriage, establishing good relations with Spain by taking as his wife Eleonora of Toledo, daughter of the Spanish Viceroy of Naples. Secure on two fronts, with a family alliance with the Hapsburgs, and with a Medici pope in Rome, Cosimo could turn to the task of making his rule manifest in architecture, statuary and painting. Like his ancestors, Old Cosimo and Lorenzo the Magnificent, he was to prove a great and intelligent patron.

In a city already full of great artistic symbols of republicanism, Cosimo was quick to recognise the importance of art and ceremony as visual expressions of the new regime. Within a short time he moved out of the old family palace and established himself and his court in the great, grim fortress of the Palazzo della Signoria, where the city council had formerly met. It was a brilliant stroke to transform in this way that time-honoured republican monument into the stronghold of the new autocracy.

The old Hall of the Great Council became the throne room. At the north end stood an imposing raised dais, the *Udienza*, upon which the ducal throne was seen against a row of niches containing statues of Cosimo himself and of his illustrious forebears carved

Cosimo I de' Medici sits enthroned among the artists, architects and craftsmen who glorified his reign in Florence. This fresco by Cosimo's court painter, Giorgio Vasari, is part of one of the ceilings in the Palazzo della Signoria, the ancient seat of the city's government. The duke, as patron, lords it over the former republic

*ABOVE: Cellini's bronze bust of the duke captures the strength of will which enabled him
to wrest power for himself from his political opponents. OPPOSITE: The duchess, Eleonora of Toledo,
looks out ambivalently from Agnolo Bronzino's mysterious likeness of her. Both works
of art capture the essence of Mannerism in Medici Florence*

by Baccio Bandinelli. Facing this obvious assertion of temporal might was a more allegorical celebration of Florentine power in the form of a great fountain façade, begun by Bartolomeo Ammanati but never completed. This vast room was to be the setting for a series of lavish theatrical entertainments and court masques known as *intermedi.* Opera, serious and comic drama, mock-battles by land and sea and glorious music united to celebrate and symbolize the young duke's power.

Throughout the 1540s Cosimo's architects and designers were hard at work on the palace, creating both public and private interiors in the latest style. The grand classicism of the High Renaissance was at this time evolving in the hands of clever young artists, who played with the

rules to create more vivid and theatrical forms, not only in architecture and decoration, but also in sculpture and the visual arts. Foremost amongst the practitioners of this new style, known as Mannerism, were the painter Agnolo Bronzino and the sculptors Benvenuto Cellini and Giambologna.

It is through the eyes of Bronzino that we most readily glimpse Cosimo's world. One of the most glamorous images of any great woman of the period is a portrait of the Duchess Eleonora, who wears in this compelling picture a sumptuous gown of brown velvet with an intricate interlaced pattern: the very dress in which she was arrayed in her tomb. Bronzino had also created the standard likeness of the duke, a half-length portrait in white armour: a cold and formal work which Cosimo seems to have preferred as a likeness to the quirky and expressive bust which had been cast in bronze as a trial piece by Cellini.

The cool and calculating duke must have found the mercurial and conceited Cellini a difficult character, but it is a mark of his discernment that he recognised in the boastful sculptor the one artist who could produce, in the *Perseus,* a large-scale sculpture that could stand beside Michelangelo's republican *David* and sweeten with its grace the hard message of autocracy. Cellini's statue is wrought with all the cunning of the goldsmith's art, and is definitively a product of princely

indulgence, yet it was made to be set outside the Palazzo as part of a carefully placed sequence of public sculptures. Cosimo had consulted the great Michelangelo himself in planning the rearrangement of the Piazza della Signoria. The master's elaborate scheme proved prohibitively expensive, but his plan of a sculptural axis was followed with a number of major works, culminating in the great equestrian monument to Cosimo.

Cosimo fulfilled enthusiastically the obligation of a Renaissance prince to assemble a cabinet of treasures. From the mid-1540s he collected medals and other small objects which in 1559 found a home in the *Tessoretto,* which he had commanded to be hollowed out, literally, from the walls of the Palazzo. However, by this time work was already in hand on a new and grandiose palace quite different from the former seat of republican government.

As early as 1549 Eleonora, disliking the gloom of the medieval castle, had bought from the Pitti family their mansion on the hillside on the far bank of the river Arno. Part of its appeal lay in the open aspect of the site and in the opportunity for creating a pleasure garden. After 15 years of architectural works and decorative embellishment the palace was ready. There Cosimo and Eleonora passed their days in the observation of public ceremony on a grand scale and in the pursuit of a more private and cultivated leisure. It was a new model of European princely life.

ABOVE: This cameo carving representing Cosimo, Eleonora and their children is the work of the talented carver, de' Rossi, and is one of many objects carved in semiprecious stone in the great Medici collections. OPPOSITE: PERSEUS WITH HEAD OF MEDUSA symbolises the triumphalism of Cosimo's regime. The great bronze figure is a Cellini masterpiece and was commissioned to stand in the Loggia dei Lanze

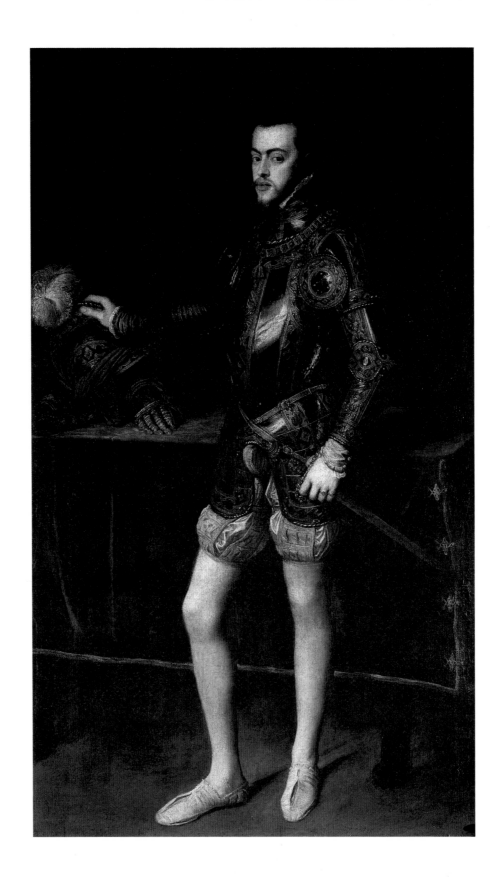

PHILIP II

Strong fathers do not always breed strong sons. Charles V, Holy Roman Emperor and therefore ruler of half the Old and New Worlds, had established the Hapsburg hegemony throughout Europe by a charismatic combination of wise and humane rule and military determination. His only legitimate son, Philip, was by contrast authoritarian - cool and calculating where his father had been magnanimous. When, in 1555, Charles V withdrew from all temporal concerns to live out his final days in spiritual contemplation at the monastery of Yuste, he made over to the young Philip all his Spanish and Burgundian dominions, one half of that great empire which had seemed so unassailable.

It was Philip's tragedy that his long reign was to be conducted against a background of political turmoil and religious revolution. The rise of Protestantism in Europe challenged all religious and social order, driving Philip to take up arms as the champion of Catholic orthodoxy. At first, ruling from his father's old capital at Brussels, the political situation seemed full of promise, and Philip was able to cultivate his interests in the arts which had first been stimulated by his early travels in Italy and the Low Countries. When war broke out with France in 1557 Philip rapidly secured a great victory at the battle of St Quentin, fought on the feast-day of St Lawrence, in whose honour he immediately vowed to found a monastery. In less than two years he had pressed home his military advantage and dictated terms to the French at the Treaty of Cateau-Cambrésis.

With the death of Charles V in 1558 Philip took the momentous decision to return to Spain, where he had grown up. Making Madrid his new capital, he began to plan the great building which would serve as monastery, palace, government offices, and royal necropolis. El Escorial was begun in 1562 in a spirit of Catholic triumphalism; during the next 30 years it would become the grim fortress of an embattled faith, from which the Most Catholic Monarch sought to impose his iron will, governing, as he liked to claim, 'half the world with two inches of paper.'

Set high amid the bare hills above Madrid, the Escorial is a great, bleak complex of hard grey stone. Its dignity and symmetry are less the creation of

Titian, the greatest portrait painter of his day, in this incisive
characterisation of Philip II, seeks out the private man behind the autocratic mask.
Hesitant but stubborn, quiet but determined, this was the man who
'governed half the world with two inches of paper'

ABOVE: Philip in old age, portayed in a profile cameo of coloured wax, a favourite medium for small, informal portraits. OPPOSITE: The austerity of the king of Spain was strangely at odds with his taste in pictures. His passion for the works of Titian, conceived at an early age, led him to commission in later life a series of sensuous allegories such as this VENUS WITH THE ORGAN PLAYER in which Philip himself is depicted at the keyboard

its architects, Juan Bautista de Toledo and Juan de Herrera, than an expression of Philip's own determination to impose upon every aspect of his realm the sober, strict regime of the Counter-Reformation. To Philip the classicism of the High Renaissance represented an ideal of order as appealing as the dogmas of the Catholic Church. Thus at a time when, throughout Europe, Mannerist architects were experimenting with extravagant forms that bor-

dered on the perverse, Philip directed his builders to eschew novelty and reserve all richness and ornament for the sombre splendours of the royal pantheon and chapel.

At the heart of the Escorial, next to the chapel, lie Philip's own apartments, whose modest scale and simple decoration provide another clue to the king's complex character, in which excessive piety and inverted egotism were equally strongly marked. Here Philip slept in a narrow bed from which he could look down upon the high altar of his great foundation. This bedroom and the tiny office next to it were the focus of Philip's daily life. There were neither rich carpets nor costly tapestries, but instead, an austere background of tiled and whitewashed walls. Here hung a collection of pictures, chosen by Philip for their religious themes but nevertheless selected with the sure eye of a connoisseur of painting.

For the altarpiece of his new chapel Philip turned to one of the great Italian masters, Titian, whose work he had admired since his first meeting with the artist many years before. Titian, the greatest of the Venetian painters of the High Renaissance, represented the same artistic propriety that Philip admired in architecture. He had painted for

Philip, when he first came to the Spanish throne, a magnificent series of classical subjects, illustrating themes from the poetry of Ovid. Philip also commissioned from him the elegant if eccentric painting of *Venus with the Organ Player*.

These pictures which have neither reigious nor moral messages represent the most relaxed and self-indulgent aspects of Philip's artistic tastes. The darker side of the personality of this driven man is represented by his obsessional interest in the fantastical works of the late fifteenth-century Flemish painter, Hieronymus Bosch. Bosch's paintings are an extraordinary survival into the modern age of an entirely late-medieval world picture. Heaven, Purgatory and Hell are minutely depicted, but it is the agonies of the damned, harried by demons, upon which the artist's weird consciousness is fixated. Philip obviously recognised in these images many aspects of his own spiritual torment, for as a leading protagonist of the Counter-Reformation he shared all Bosch's primitive fears without the panacea of absolute religious certainty. The king brought together in the Escorial the majority of Bosch's surviving works, ensuring, with the same punctilious attention to detail which he brought to his daily corre-

spondence, that he should have before his eyes every last grim scene from the artist's tortured imagination.

Though Philip could recognise and delight in the merits of Titian's pagan subjects, any religious work of art had to fulfil his exacting standards in matters of iconography, design and handling. An exquisite white marble *Crucifixion* by Benvenuto Cellini, sent to him by the Grand Duke of Tuscany, failed to satisfy the king's requirements of 'gravity' and 'decorum'. Similarly, Philip's taste was affronted by the revolutionary composition and handling of paint in the works of the young Venetian trained artist, Domenico Theotokopoulos, known from his country of birth as *El Greco*. He was summoned through the king's agent to the Spanish court and it is thought that his extraordinary painting known as the *Dream of Philip II* was painted as a presentation piece to impress his royal patron. Having initially gained Philip's favour, El Greco received a prestigious commission to paint an altarpiece for the chapel of St Maurice in the Escorial. The fevered and elongated forms of the figures and the eccentricity of the composition caused the king to reject both canvas and artist, demonstrating that in art, as in life, Philip's conscience ruled remorselessly over his sensibilities.

Philip's religious mania was reflected in his obsessive collecting of the strange pictures of the late fifteenth-century Flemish painter, Hieronymus Bosch. In this detail from the right-hand wing of the triptych called THE GARDEN OF EARTHLY DELIGHTS, *Bosch depicts in lurid detail the torments of the damned*

17TH CENTURY

THE AGE OF GRANDEUR

'Great Monarch of the World, from whose arm springs
The potency and power of kings...'

King Charles I, from the poem MAJESTY IN MISERY

el emperador Rodolfo.

RUDOLF II

Rudolf II was the Hapsburg who, in 1576, succeeded to the throne of the Holy Roman Empire. Although he had been educated for eight years at the court of his Spanish cousins, he could not have been more different: enquiring where they were orthodox, intuitive and original where they were pedantic. It was perhaps inevitable, given the scale and diversity of the Hapsburg dominions, that once Charles V had begun the process of parcelling out the eastern and Spanish territories to the various branches of his family, rivalry and distrust would follow. Rudolf, as heir to the traditional Hapsburg lands in Germany and Austria, secured as had become customary the title of emperor and the nominally elective crowns of the kingdoms of Bohemia

and Hungary. But he inherited with them nothing of the security or confidence which should have accompanied these glittering prizes.

Rudolf's world had grown out of turbulent religious controversy and appalling civil strife within the boundaries of Europe. Meanwhile, beyond the Danube the threat of Turkish invasion became a more sinister spectre. It was not only religious certainties which were now called in question. In the arts the rules of classical propriety were in disarray. In Italy artists such as Giambologna had tormented the pure forms of the High Renaissance in search of new expressive modes. Science and the study of the natural world had advanced by this time to a new level of understanding and seemed to offer an appealingly secure

foundation of verifiable facts upon which to construct a world picture.

Throughout the German states princes and rulers were giving a tangible form to this new intellectual viewpoint by forming collections of curiosities. These were objects intended to demonstrate the wonders of the natural world and the genius of artists and craftsmen. Both Rudolf's grandfather and father had begun such collections, but that formed by Rudolf himself in his new capital at Prague reflected more completely the emperor's beliefs and conception of the world. It grew over a period of 40 years into one of the most remarkable assemblages of works of art and curiosities ever brought together in one place.

It is impossible to separate Rudolf

Rudolf II was a complex man, the greatest collector of his era. He had an insatiable curiosity for and vast knowledge of the objects of the natural world, but little interest in his fellow men or understanding of their machinations. He is depicted here in a conventional pose of royal and military grandeur by a court portrait painter, Hans von Aachen

the aesthete from Rudolf the mystic. Many of the works of art made at his command employ perversity of form, bizarre materials, erotic and decadent themes and hidden symbolism to express secrets of alchemy, magic or arcane philosophy. Rudolf collected men too, in much the same way that he gathered objects, drawing to his court at the castle of Hradschin a curous circle of cunning painters, unworldly scientists and knowing charlatans, among them the celebrated English magus, Doctor John Dee.

Artists at Rudolf's court were required to follow a strict programme of iconography and subject matter. The two principle themes which they were directed to elaborate upon were first, the glorification of the Hapsburg dynasty in general and its culmination in the person of Rudolf, and second, a minutely detailed and polished representation of the more curious aspects of the natural world. Thus, the splendour of court spectacle and the self-conscious virtuosity of artists and craftsmen united to exemplify the new Mannerist style in Prague.

The key figure in this extraordinary visual world was the Milanese painter Giuseppe Arcimboldo. He had first served Rudolf's grandfather, designing masques and painting portraits: but it was with Rudolf's encouragement that he carried out the bizarre 'composite heads' on which his reputation now rests. In these strange canvases, many of which are thought to represent actual personages of the court, each head is contrived as a surreal but symbolic assemblage of fruits or books or other appropriate objects.

Rudolf tried to tempt a great many artists to travel to Prague. He failed to secure Giambologna because the Medici would not release him from Florence but the great sculptor arranged for two talented young artists, both fellow Flemings, Hans de Monte and Bartholomeus Spranger, to enter Rudolf's service. Little is known of de Monte, but Spranger became, like Arcimboldo, one of the emperor's favourite artists. He had absorbed the influence of some of the most important of the Italian Mannerists. His sinuous and sensual rendering of disconcertingly erotic scenes from the loves of the gods appealed to Rudolf's undoubted liking for the curious and mildly indecent.

It is Spranger's work that represents the most cosmopolitan aspect of Rudolphine taste. The exactitude of his

Sixteenth and seventeenth century princes demonstrated their culture by forming cabinets of curiosities and KUNSTKAMMERN, devoted respectively to the creations of nature and the cunning of the craftsman's hand. This idealised view of a KUNSTKAMMER is an ALLEGORY OF SIGHT, from a set of THE FIVE SENSES painted by Jan 'Velvet' Brueghel, originally in the collection of Rudolf II

ABOVE: *An exquisite object from Rudolf's collection: a ewer formed from a 'Seychelles nut' (Coco-de-mer shell) and elaborately mounted by the goldsmith, Schweinberger.* OPPOSITE: *The Imperial Crown is the masterpiece of Rudolf's goldsmiths. It was completed in the Imperial Workshops in Prague in 1602*

draughtsmanship and the delicious flow of his line were qualities that lent themselves very readily to reproduction in engravings, many of which were made by Rudolf's celebrated printmakers, Aegidius Sadeler and Hendrik Goltzius. Together with Lucas Killian these two extraordinary craftsmen played a leading role in the attempt to revive the reputation and rival the achievements of Germany's greatest engraver, Albrecht Dürer. Dürer, who had died in 1528, held a special place in the Hapsburg myth-

ology, for it was he who had fixed for all time the image of his patron, Rudolf's revered ancestor, the first Maximilian.

Goltzius, like the emperor, was fascinated by the mysteries of alchemy and magic. During the course of his long reign Rudolf withdrew increasingly from the perplexities of his political obligations, taking refuge among his collections in the silent and secret rooms of the so-called Spanish wing of the Hradschin. Obsessed with the mystical significance of precious stones and rare minerals, he

preferred to lose himself in charting the future through the stars rather than confront the present. His seclusion became legendary and the fabric of the state began to crumble around him. Thus the scholar-emperor, happy among his books like Shakespeare's Prospero, was finally supplanted in 1611 by his more worldly brother, Matthias. In less than a year Rudolf died, with the belief that his remarkable collections would be preserved intact as a monument to his rule more enduring than any earthly crown.

MARIE DE' MEDICI & LOUIS XIII

Had Henri IV not driven out from the Louvre on 14th May 1610 to meet his fate at the hand of the assassin, Ravaillac, France might have enjoyed a period of greater stability under his wise and even-handed rule. As it was, the sudden death of the man who had brought peace and a degree of religious toleration to the troubled nation, left the reins of power in the wilful but uncertain grip of his widow, Marie de' Medici, mother of the nine-year-old Louis XIII.

Marie de' Medici came of a family that well understood the twin virtues of power and money. Lacking any great imagination or intellectual distinction, she nonetheless relished the central role in which she found herself cast as regent for the boy king. The queen was vain and stubborn and her chief concern during the Minority was to secure her own position, which she did in the main by insisting upon the strict observance of all honours that she considered due to her. As a patron of the arts her attitude was not dissimilar; she understood the importance of display as an instrument of statecraft and the desirability of maintaining a public reputation as a connoisseur.

As a child Louis had been beaten regularly at his father's command, in order to toughen him; a treatment which, as often is the case, had quite the opposite effect. The young king was nervous, neurotic and intensely sensitive. He was extremely religious and highly responsive to the stimulus of the visual arts. He had a love of music and his personal accomplishments included a talent for composition and performance; he also drew well and showed considerable taste as a connoisseur. In all of this he resembled a good deal his brother-in-law, Charles I of England. But where Charles was able, for 16 years, to cultivate his role as royal patron, Louis was, from the first, obliged to concentrate his resources upon securing his own throne. The early years of his reign were dominated by the struggle, first to wrest power from his mother, which he did in 1617, and then to retain it in the face of her intrigues and outright hostilities.

Given the turbulence of the first part of Louis's reign it is not surprising that he had little time for artistic achievements. It was not until 1624 that negotiations with Spain and England brought greater stability in France's international relations. In the same year Louis brought back into the royal council that

LOUIS XIII CROWNED BY VICTORY, a bold allegorical likeness by Philippe de Champaigne, who came to France as Rubens's assistant when, in 1621, the great master was summoned to work on his series of paintings of the life of Marie de' Medici. Cardinal Richelieu considered Rubens an agent of the King of Spain, but liked de Champaigne whom he advanced to become Court Painter

fascinating and ruthless figure, Cardinal Richelieu. The cardinal's over-riding ambition was the development of a political system that would ensure the strength of the nation and the unassailable pre-eminence of the crown.

France and its capital in the 1620s were in aspect still largely unchanged since medieval times. Richelieu was ambitious for his monarch to rule over a modern state, one supplied with all the graces and virtues of painting, architecture and letters. But the arts could not be allowed to flourish without careful guidance. The cardinal sought to establish a new golden age in France through the creation of academies of art and literature. At the same time, far-reaching programmes of urban planning and magnificent building began to transform the face of the old city of Paris.

The first tentative beginnings of a coherent design for for the city centre had been essayed under Henri IV, when the enchanting arcaded square of the Place des Vosges was laid out. This was completed in Louis's reign, and became a fashionable meeting place. A fine new bridge, linking the Place Dauphine with the Samaritaine across the tip of the old Île de la Cité in one bold gesture improved the communications between the cluttered ancient districts at the heart of the town and introduced the exciting concept of scenographic urban planning on the Roman scale.

The architectural achievements of this period include the two great churches in the newly introduced Jesuit Baroque style: that of the Jesuit fathers themselves in the Rue St Antoine, close to the Marais, and Notre Dame des Victoires, completed in 1629 in thanksgiving for the restitution of unity and security at the fall of La Rochelle.

The queen mother, whilst still regent, had embarked upon the creation of a new royal residence, the Palais du Luxembourg; it was built to the designs of Salomon de Brosse, after the Italian fashion, in an open space surrounded by gardens on the left bank of the Seine. Standing on the outskirts of Paris it was in situation and appearance calculated to remind Marie de' Medici of her home at the Pitti Palace in Florence. But she was to enjoy the nobility of de Brosse's architecture, and the soothing sycophancy of Rubens's great cycle of paintings of highlights from her own life, which she had commissioned as decoration, for only a few short years. In 1630 her final power struggle with Cardinal Richelieu for influence over the king resulted in her flight and exile from France.

At the Louvre Louis commissioned new building works, demolishing the old central court of the royal palace. Vastly enlarged new wings were begun on the north and west, culminating in the Pavillon de l'Horloge of 1625, with its decoration enriched with caryatids by the sculptor Sarrazin. Work on the Louvre continued throughout Louis's reign, and in 1639 Nicolas Poussin, the greatest classical painter of the period, was recalled from Rome to decorate the king's new state-rooms.

Richelieu was no less busy, creating close by the new Palais Cardinal, a magnificent complex of buildings, which erased a whole squalid maze of ancient tenements and substituted the handsome sequence of regular façades and arcaded courts known today as the Palais Royal.

While Philippe de Champaigne's state portraits of the king convey the official image of the French monarchy, strong and victorious, Louis was in fact sickly as a child and grew to be a valetudinarian adult. The ill-health which dogged him throughout his 42 years of life made him

*A bird's-eye view, by an unknown artist, of the celebrations held for the union of Louis XIII
and Anne of Austria. The Place des Vosges (formerly the Place Royale) was begun under Henri IV and
completed by Marie de' Medici in 1612, the vast arcaded square forming one of the grandest
urban cityscapes of its era. The tall, central building at the left is the Pavillon du Roi; it is echoed by
the Pavillon de la Reine on the north side, to the right*

*ABOVE: The so-called Mirror of Marie de' Medici, a sumptuous
object set with gems and rare agates typifies the queen's extravagant tastes.
OPPOSITE: MARIE DE' MEDICI CROWNED BY VICTORY, one of the great
series of canvases commissioned from Rubens in 1621 for the decoration of
the Queen's Palais du Luxembourg*

vulnerable to the more dubious nostrums of the time and led him to a dependence upon quasi-religious talismans. He set great store by religious images as a protection against disease, but as a sophisticated patron of the arts he surrounded himself with icons of the highest quality. Of the many paintings which he aquired, he valued most highly the moving torch-lit scene, by Georges de la Tour, of the martyred Saint Sebastian, presented to him by the artist as a prophylactic against plague. Perhaps this solemn image, rather than more pompous and vain glorious allegories, most clearly reflects the mind of a man whose character bridges the gulf between medieval credulity and modern sophistication.

CHARLES I

Although all monarchs have used art and architecture for the purposes of propaganda, far fewer have been truly passionate connoisseurs. First amongst this select band must be Charles I, 'the greatest amateur of paintings amongst the princes of the world' as he was called by the great Flemish artist Rubens. His enthusiasms as a collector and patron brought to England some of the noblest classical architecture and many of the greatest works of art assembled at any European court before or since.

Charles was a shy and scholarly boy, fastidious, and thus instinctively at odds with the grosser aspects of life at the court of his father, James I. He lived his early years in the shadow of his brilliant elder brother Henry, Prince of Wales, whose own circle of artists, collectors and men of letters must have been so much more congenial to the sensitive Charles. With the tragic, early death of his brother in 1612, Charles became heir not only to the thrones of England and Scotland, but also to that vital artistic and intellectual world that Prince Henry had created.

Although Charles had shown, even as a child, a precocious delight in the visual arts, it was in the company of two great courtiers that he refined his taste and enlarged his horizons to include both the works of antiquity and the finest productions of contemporary European artists. George Villiers, Duke of Buckingham, was James I's favourite, but also a close friend of Prince Charles, accompanying him to Spain in 1623 in pursuit of a marriage alliance. Though Charles failed to capture the hand of the Infanta, he developed with Buckingham's encouragement an enduring passion for the work of Italian painters, such as Titian, many of whose masterpieces had been acquired by Philip IV, and made the first of his many great coups as a collector, the purchase of the celebrated series of tapestry designs by Raphael. These cartoons remain one of the great treasures of the British royal collection.

Charles's second important mentor was Thomas Howard, Earl of Arundel, who had travelled extensively in Italy buying antique statuary and studying the work of painters and architects of the High Renaissance. It was he who first encouraged Inigo Jones to develop those novel Italian ideas

In his portraits of Charles I, aesthete, king and martyr, Sir Anthony Van Dyck's
extraordinary sensitivity to psychological nuances allowed him to capture precisely his royal patron's
complex character. We see Charles, something of the dandy and with a connoisseur's
love of beauty, yet flawed by a fatal human frailty

ABOVE: A VIEW OF OLD WHITEHALL, by Danckerts. The grand classical façade in pale stone of the Banqueting House stands in marked contrast to the jumble of older palace buildings to the south. OPPOSITE: Among Charles's greatest artistic purchases were the nine large canvases of the TRIUMPH OF CAESAR by Andrea Mantegna

which would transform English building and impose upon the narrow Tudor streets of Westminster a gleaming vision of classical architecture to stand as a monument to the Stuart dynasty.

The Palace of Whitehall was essentially still a medieval maze of irregular half-timbered wings and corridors. This gabled royal anthill had grown up gradually and without order. Prince Charles, inspired by Jones's clever drawings, encouraged his father to commission a great new Banqueting House to replace one which had burned down in 1619. Work began before James's death but with Charles's accession in 1625 the project took on an additional significance. The young king commanded Inigo Jones to crown his architectural achievement by devising a scheme of ceiling paintings to glorify the peace and prosperity established under King James's rule. It is a measure of Charles's taste and ambition as a patron that he was determined that

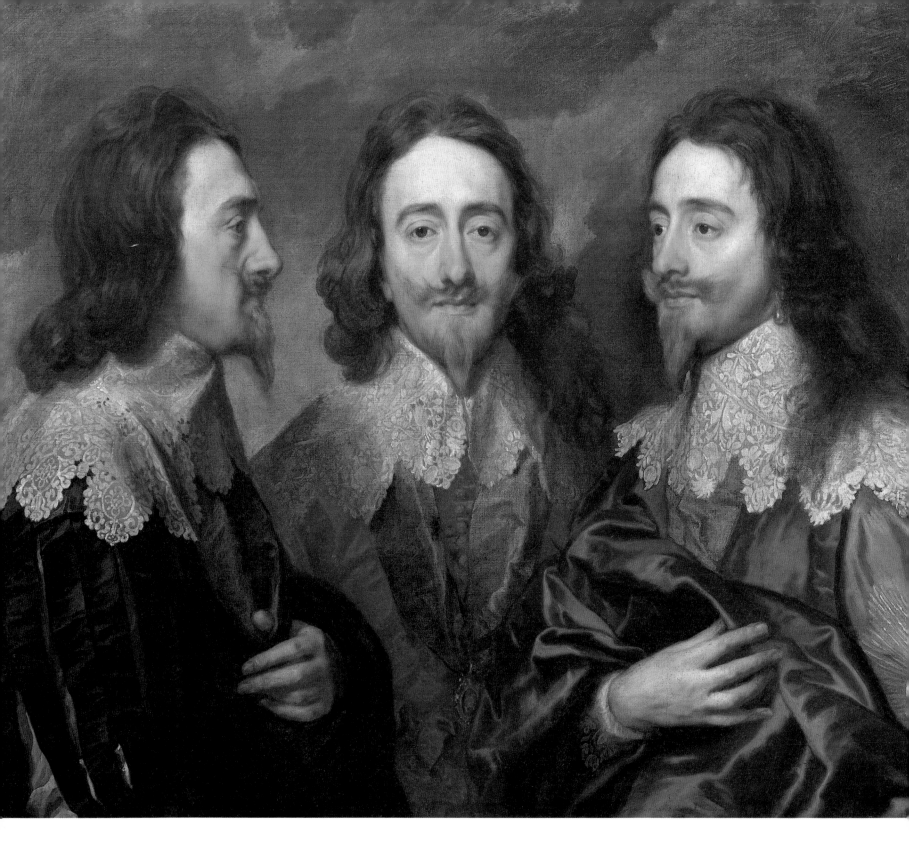

this noble decorative scheme should be entrusted to the foremost painter in Europe, Peter Paul Rubens.

Charles's passion for pictures and sculpture led him to cast envious eyes on the collections of the Gonzaga Dukes of Mantua, which were famed throughout Europe for their magnificence. Rumours abounded that financial ruin faced the Duchy of Mantua and that these fabled masterpieces could be secured in return for ready cash. Charles's own finances relied heavily upon credit, but recognising the chance of establishing himself, at a stroke, as one of the greatest of princely collectors, he borrowed over £18,000 from the moneylender, Burlamachi. In return for this considerable sum, gradually over the next decade Charles took possession of all the best Mantuan pieces, including ancient and contemporary sculptures, and an astonishing array of paintings, including such major works as Andrea Mantegna's nine great canvases of the *Triumph of Caesar*, the *Entombment of Christ* by Titian, and Correggio's sensuously painted allegory of love, *Mercury instructing Cupid before Venus*.

Charles was a small man but as a king in his own court he was determined to cut a noble figure. The court masques devised by Ben Jonson and Inigo Jones presented images of divine and heroic majesty. No less crucial were the painted and carved portraits of the king, which enshrined Charles's self-image as a generous ruler and God's representative on earth. Anthony Van Dyck, the brilliant pupil of Rubens, brought to English court portraiture the sumptuous Baroque style of his master, but added to that extravagance a psychological penetration that fixed for all time the image of the king and his cavaliers.

Perhaps the most poignant image of the doomed Caroline court is Van Dyck's triple portrait of Charles, which was painted to serve as a model from which the great Italian Baroque sculptor, Bernini, executed a vivid marble bust, subsequently destroyed. This more than any other work of art answered Charles's desire to assume the role of an international patron and connoisseur. When, in 1649, the final act of Charles's tragedy was played upon the executioner's scaffold outside a window of the Banqueting House, there was a bitter irony in the fact that it was the king's extravagant artistic purchases which had first brought him to the brink of political ruin. The very image of kingship which he had believed would establish his absolute power was thrown down by the iconoclasts and regicides of a philistine parliament.

Charles I and Lord Arundel were the first connoisseurs of sculpture in England. In addition to buying antique works, Charles desired to have a portrait bust of himself carved by the greatest living sculptor, Bernini. Seeking to win his favour the Pope commissioned such a bust. Van Dyck's masterly triple portrait of the King was sent to Bernini in Rome as a pattern from which to work. Tragically, the bust was lost in the fire of Whitehall, 1698

CHRISTINA OF SWEDEN

Between 1618 and 1648 politics and patronage in continental Europe were conducted in the shadow of that great conflict, known as the Thirty Years War, which pitted the forces of Hapsburg Catholic absolutism against a shifting alliance of Protestant crusaders, beleaguered mercantile cities and political opportunists. Among the latter Gustavus Adolphus of Sweden, the 'Lion of the North', was beyond doubt the most important player. As Swedish troops swept down through Europe their fearsome reputation for pillage led even such cities as were spared the fire and the sword to offer up treasures in the hope of appeasing the rapacious Swedish warlord.

The Thirty Years War devastated large tracts of northern Europe and the systems of government which had for generations dominated European politics. During that upheaval the cultural imperatives which had, through the rule of the house of Hapsburg, continued to direct patronage of the arts, were replaced by a new and curiously violent acquisitiveness which had little to do with the subtle appreciation of art and everything to do with the prestige of plunder.

Gustavus Adolphus cared nothing for art as an end in itself: every painting and piece of sculpture sent back to Stockholm was for him a trophy of martial victory. The early years of his daughter, Christina, must have been dominated by an awareness of the continuous stream of treasures that poured into the royal palaces from despoiled cities and monasteries throughout Germany.

In 1632 the king was killed in the hour of victory at the battle of Lutzen, whilst in the throes of his campaigns. Christina was still a child, and it was to be nearly a decade before she achieved her majority. Meanwhile, the wars continued. In 1639 the Swedes laid siege to the city of Prague, the treasure-house of the late Emperor Rudolf II. But Rudolf's remarkable collections had been hidden by the imperial chamberlain, and so the Swedes were frustrated of their prize. When, in 1644, Christina came of age and was able to take into her own hands the direction of her armies, she was determined that the Rudolphine collections should be hers.

The two generals in charge of the Swedish forces were Charles Gustavus of Zweibrücken, the queen's own cousin, and Count Königsmark. In 1648 they

After her abdication and journey to Rome in 1654, the portraits of Christina of Sweden become fixed in a standard pattern, shewing her like an sensuous allegorical figure, hair loosed and wrapped in a rich gown which slides to reveal the shoulder. This version by Falck shows the queen's imperious character tinged with a haunting look of introspection

invaded Prague and prepared to take the city. Meanwhile, the European powers, Sweden amongst them, were preparing to seek a peaceful end to the crippling wars. Almost upon the eve of the signing of the Peace of Westphalia Christina wrote to Charles at Prague, urging him to 'Take good care, to send me the library and the works of art that are there: for you know that they are the only things for which I care.'

These 'things' included some of the most remarkable masterpieces of Renaissance and Mannerist art from Rudolf's collection. Dürer's *Adam* and *Eve* and Jan Massys's *Venus* were among the pictures that Königsmark brought back, together with, the superb equestrian statue of Rudolf by Giambologna. The great library of printed books and manuscripts which Rudolf had assembled was one of the queen's chief targets, for she had an insatiable appetite for learning of all kinds. However, her intellectual yearning was not matched by her aesthetic sensibility. One of the glories of the imperial library was the large number of books which retained their original medieval and Renaissance bindings. These were ruthlessly ripped off in order to lighten the loads of the clumsy wagons that rolled northward to Stockholm bearing the spoils.

At a stroke Christina transformed the Swedish royal collections. It was said of the palace in Stockholm before the arrival of the first pillaged pictures that there had been but a single painting there, and that Swedish. Now there were enough works of art and rare volumes to fill the royal apartments, and still leave rich pickings for Königsmark and the queen's other nobles, such as Count Wrangel. Meanwhile, the royal librarians pursued a brisk trade selling 'unwanted' books from the collection to the ignorant but aspirant palace-building Swedish nobles.

The queen's own attitude to intellectual pursuits was ambivalent. The crucial figure in her lonely upbringing had been Count Axel Oxenstierna, chancellor of the realm and, from 1632, regent: a man whose wisdom and statecraft caused him to be likened to those French princes of the Church and political geniuses, Richelieu and Mazarin. Oxenstierna devised a curriculum which included languages, art, music and philosophy. Christina emerged from this regime as a fiercely independent bluestocking, impatient of the trammels of monarchy, and as greedy in her desire for the fruits of

In this highly unusual depiction of a royal patron, Queen Christina has commanded her painter to show her among the scholars and savants with whom she delighted to surround herself, studying and disputing upon a wide range of subjects. The queen is seated at the table, attended by Descartes, the greatest of the intellectual figures who accepted Christina's summons

ABOVE: VENUS, *painted in 1561 by Jan Massys; one of the finest paintings
from the collection of the Emperor Rudolf II looted by Count Königsmark from Prague in 1648.
OPPOSITE: A reconstruction of Queen Christina's coronation coach
drawn by six richly caparisoned horses*

learning as her father had been for the spoils of war.

She relished learned discourse so greatly that, when the French philosopher Réné Descartes came to Stockholm at her express request, the poor man was hounded by his would-be disciple, who forced him to rise before dawn to give her tutorials at five o'clock. The cold and damp brought Descartes down with pneumonia, so that Christina may be said to have talked him into an early grave. Though she surrounded herself with scholars, philosophers and astronomers this was not a court to

rival that of Rudolf in Prague. She had been able to steal the objects and the books which had been a part of that rich intellectual world of study and experiment, but she could not purloin the ideas, nor recreate in the dour North the atmosphere of enlightened humanism that had existed in Prague.

Within a few short years of her majority, in 1644, Christina had realised that she was temperamentally unsuited to marriage and that her intellectual and religious yearnings would ultimately make Sweden a prison to her. Her unwillingness to be fettered meant that it was not

until 1650, when the issue of succession was resolved by the adoption of her cousin Charles as her heir, that the elaborate plans for her coronation could proceed. This great ceremony, ten years in the making, was the most extravagant in Sweden's history. By a twist of fate it was also an empty gesture, for only four years later Christina stunned Europe by embracing the Catholic faith, abdicating her throne and embarking upon a cultural and spiritual pilgrimage to Rome, where she ended her days in luxury and aesthetic indulgence.

LOUIS XIV

No ruler has ever made style and luxury such conspicuous and effective tools of his power as did Louis XIV of France. The egotism of the king was fostered from his early years by the devotion of his mother, Anne of Austria; whilst constant political insecurity cultivated in Louis a lifelong independence and determination. Almost as soon as he came to the throne, in 1643 on the death of his father Louis XIII, the boy king, aged only five, became the centre of a web of intrigue and power-play. His mother, as regent, wisely made common cause with her former political adversary, Cardinal Mazarin.

Mazarin had inherited from his brilliant and devious mentor, Cardinal Richelieu, a vision of a France dominant in Europe under an all-powerful king.

Louis believed in this as he believed in himself, absolutely. Following the tumultuous years of the Fronde, in which overweening nobles and a greedy bourgeoisie allied against the rule of the crown, stability was reestablished and confirmed by the great ceremony of the sixteen-year-old king's coronation at Rheims.

Mazarin chose carefully a group of ministers to advise and support the king as he established Louis's authority. Chief amongst them was the superintendent of finance and minister of state, Nicolas Fouquet. It was Fouquet who, in building the great château of Vaux-le-Vicomte, revealed to an envious monarch the uses of magnificence. Like Wolsey before him, Fouquet abused the privileges of office flagrantly, amassing

a fortune and building lavishly. It was he who first brought together for a single project that great triumvirate of designers, Louis Le Vau as architect, the artist Charles Le Brun as decorator and Andre Le Nôtre, the most innovative garden-maker of his age.

On a fateful night in August 1661 Fouquet gave a lavish entertainment to placate his master's envy. But Louis moved with the ruthlessness of a child snatching another's toy, and before the night was out Fouquet was in chains and his house and all its treasures in the hands of the king.

The seizure of Vaux proved to be a turning point in Louis's life, for he learned from the episode the valuable lesson that art and architecture can be potent manifestations of power. It had already become clear to him that, to

LOUIS XIV AND HIS HEIRS, by Nicolas de Largilliere. Though grouped as a delightful, informal conversation piece this picture makes a grand dynastic statement. The busts are those of Louis XIV's grandfather, Henri IV and father, Louis XIII. The King, seated, is attended by his heir, the Grand Dauphin, behind him. His eldest grandson the Duke of Burgundy stands to the right, whilst a nurse presents his son, the Duke of Brittany, elder brother of the future Louis XV

The richness and grandeur of Versailles set a style and standard in palace building to which most rulers aspired for two centuries. The bedchamber of the King (ABOVE) was furnished with the most sumptuous hangings in cloth-of-gold. The celebrated GALERIE DES GLACES (OPPOSITE) in addition to the vast cost of its mirror-glass and crystal chandeliers was originally ornamented with silver furniture

maintain stability, he needed to keep the nobility away from Paris, but nonetheless under his watchful eye. The ideal solution lay in obliging them to dance attendance upon him and to dissipate their potentially dangerous wealth in ever more costly extravagances. A new focus for court life was needed. Vaux-le-Vicomte would supply the model, but the new palace at Versailles must outshine it, as does the sun the stars.

In the firmament of his new court Louis deliberately cast himself in the role of *le Roi-Soleil*, the brilliant Sun King who is the source of all life, light and harmony. Like other monarchs Louis understood the vital significance of Baroque spectacle as a means of conveying an image of majesty. Not only did he star in the series of magnificent symbolic ballets and masques staged at Versailles: he made every hour of his day into a scene in an unceasing royal drama. Each was strictly codified and choreographed. From his first rising, the *levée*, when the senior nobleman present proffered the royal shirt, through to the king's supper and retiring, all was carried out before an appreciative audience and to the music of Lully and Rameau.

Versailles had been no more than a simple hunting lodge of Louis XIII until, in the early 1660s, Louis began to aggrandize it under the guidance of Le Vau. By the 1670s the king's conception of the château had grown in scale to match his political pretensions. Versailles became a new Olympus with the king as Zeus, a temple of the muses in which he might play Apollo; and as France came increasingly to dominate the European field it was also the triumphant home of Mars. The king's mistresses were portrayed as nymphs and dryads or as goddesses such as Venus or Diana. Thus Versailles became not only a palace and a stage, but an allegorical realisation of the king's real achievements and fantastical dreams.

The original brick and stone façades of the handsome château of the 1660s were gradually encased by Le Vau in monumental stonework designed in a massive and symmetrical classical style touched with the exuberance of the Baroque. Spreading out in sumptuous elaboration from these great walls lay the formal gardens. Geometrical parterres spread like richly figured carpets across terraces decorated, under Le Brun's direction, with statues and urns. Beyond these gardens great avenues stretch to the horizon, interspersed with long canals of still water and

foaming fountain basins in which the sculptors' skills vied with the power of tumbling waters. Le Nôtre devised the landscaping of the vast park, but the end result is equally a tribute to the capability of Le Brun.

Louis's military campaigns had culminated triumphantly in the Treaty of Nijmegen in 1678. From that date he was able to pour ever more money and resources into his beloved Versailles. Le Vau having died in 1670, it fell to a new architect, Jules Hardouin-Mansart, to mastermind the creation of the great central suite of state-rooms. The Salle de Guerre commemorates the treaty and has, as the overwhelming centrepiece to Le Brun's decoration, a vast relief of the king as victorious general on horseback carved by Antoine Coysevox, the royal sculptor. Though extraordinarily sumptuous with variegated marbles and heavy gilding, the Salle de Guerre is only an anteroom to the unparalleled magnificence of the Galerie des Glaces, celebrated throughout Europe and envied by lesser monarchs.

At the heart of the palace lay the original State Drawing Room. In 1701 the king determined that this room, with its commanding view across the great central courtyard, should

*The art of painting portrait miniatures in enamel colours was perfected
in France during the reign of Louis XIV, the greatest exponent of
the medium being Jean Petitot I. This portrait of the king, which is highly
characteristic of his manner, has a pretty, elaborately embossed frame
which is contemporary with the image*

become his bedchamber. The decorations of this late room are among the richest executed at Versailles during the reign of Louis XIV. From the lavishly gilded cove a figure of France watched over the sleeping king. The royal bed was hung, as were the walls, with textiles brocaded with heavy gold thread, and precious marbles, ormolu and rock crystal reflected light from the tall windows, the very glazing-bars of which were gilded. Amidst all this the king might well have considered himself immortal. However, when in 1715, a few days before his seventy-seventh birthday he expired in this room, the monument to Bourbon absolutism which was Versailles lived on to feed the pretensions of his successors.

CHARLES II

The tremendous charm which Charles II exercised over his court and his subjects was so potent that it engendered an enduring legend. The image of the 'merry monarch', extravagant, dissipated and luxurious, has all but obscured the true character and achievements of this shrewd statesman and Maecenas.

In 1660 a cabal of disaffected Puritan notables and patient Cavaliers seized the political initiative and brought about the popular Restoration of the monarchy. The return of King Charles II to his rightful inheritance was a remarkable event, for no European ruler had ever mounted a throne which had previously been legally abolished. The new king was very much his father's son: a man of taste and sensibility. But where his father's shyness and unease had dis-

tanced him from his people and ultimately proved to be his undoing, the son's open and gregarious manner flattered courtiers, fascinated women and made the people love him.

During the bleak years of the Commonwealth the royal palaces, under Oliver Cromwell's direction, had been stripped, the spaces let out and their precious contents sold off. Charles began immediately upon the great task of reconstructing the Stuart fortunes. Artistically he responded to the seductive embellishments of the richly sensuous European Baroque style. In this he revealed the influence of his years of waiting in exile at the courts of his royal cousins. All the show and splendour which had been denied him as an exiled prince he was determined to enjoy as a monarch.

Charles's ambitious building projects at times threatened to outstrip his finances, but were always tempered by a sound political instinct. Thus at Greenwich, where he renovated the old Queen's House for the Queen Mother, Henrietta Maria, he also planned a great new palace to be designed by John Webb, Inigo Jones's heir. This was to have been the realisation of Charles's father's dream of a vast new riverside residence, but only one wing, that now called the Charles II Block, was completed before the disasters of 1665 and 1666, the Plague and Great Fire of London, made the rebuilding of the capital the overriding priority for the king's architects.

For at least one man the destruction of the old city was not regarded as a tragedy. Christopher Wren, a bright and

CHARLES II PRESENTED WITH A PINEAPPLE. Several versions of this curious picture dating from the late 1670s exist. Traditionally held to represent John Rose, the Royal Gardener, offering his master the first fruit grown in England, these details are now in question. It is certainly a telling likeness of the King in his latter years, dressed in the sober informal clothes which he came to favour

Sir Christopher Wren's first scheme for a new, domed cathedral was made as early as May 1666, before the Fire, but the design caused considerable controversy. The 'Great Model', ordered by Wren and completed in August 1674 represents his revised and considerably aggrandized design for St Paul's. But further argument ensued and the agreed design, more traditional and 'English' in conception was only finalised and a start made on the building several years later

ingenious Oxford don, had already shown himself to be a promising designer. When a Royal Commission was appointed to determine the shape of the new centre of London, he was inevitably consulted, first on the rebuilding of St Paul's Cathedral and subsequently upon the whole design of the capital.

Wren had, like the king, been to France, and in Paris he had been inspired by the public works being carried forward under Louis XIV's chief minister, Colbert. He proposed to Charles a city built of brick and stone, set along wide airy streets, and, as its glorious focus, a great new cathedral. The earliest plans for this were hampered by interfering bureaucrats and clergy, but Wren rapidly modified his authorised design until his conception of a great domed temple on the continental Baroque model was revealed.

Though Wren's grandiose urban vision was never to be fully realised, the architect and his king were both preoccupied for a decade with the city and its cathedral. Only in the 1670s did Charles once more turn to his personal building projects, again striking a delicate balance between national duty and private indulgence. At Windsor from

Of all the 'beauties' of the court of Good King Charles painted by Sir Peter Lely,
none seems to have inspired his pencil to such a degree as Nell Gwynn.
The most beguiling of all the king's mistresses, she is depicted here, for the delectation
of her royal master, as Venus, attended by her son, the infant
Duke of St Albans who personifies Cupid

ABOVE: An eighteenth-century view from the river of the Chelsea Hospital, founded by Charles II for the care of wounded and aged soldiers, the Chelsea Pensioners. OPPOSITE: THE KING'S YACHT EXCHANGING SALUTES, by Willem Van der Velde the Younger. Charles's own yacht was the handsomest vessel of its class and often figures prominently in the newly fashionable painted sea pieces of the day

1675 onwards an elaborate campaign of works was overseen by the king's surveyor, Hugh May, which turned the derelict medieval castle into a splendid toy fort with richly Baroque interiors. The great project of the 1680s was the foundation by the river in Chelsea of a military hospital in emulation of Louis XIV's Invalides in Paris. Wren was again the presiding genius.

By contrast with his grand official schemes, Charles's private building projects, the little palaces at Winchester and near the racecourse at Newmarket, begun for his own amusement, progressed slowly and were ultimately abandoned.

Perhaps one reason why the king's own schemes so often fizzled out lay in his short lease of interest. Charles was rarely able to keep to one subject for very long and his love of pleasure and lightness of conscience tally exactly with the picture of worldly and fascinating frivolities painted by the Restoration dramatists. In the plays of Wycherley and Congreve we see a society of foppish men and bright and wicked women such as clustered like moths around the brilliance of Charles's throne. The king's love of pretty women was legendary and the artistic record of his conquests survives in the great gallery of overtly seductive portraits made of the royal mistresses by Sir Peter Lely.

In popular history the king's most celebrated liaison was with the actress Nell Gwynn, who was a popular attraction at the Drury Lane theatre. The quality of her performances and the talk of

the town concerning her dalliance with the king were recorded with relish by the busybody, bureaucrat and diarist, Samuel Pepys. Pepys was in the thick of government and court life by virtue of his role as secretary to the Admiralty, for if there was one thing that delighted the king more than a pretty face it was the graceful lines of a new ship.

Throughout Charles's reign the ever-present threat of Dutch sea power made the building up of the navy a vital plank of national policy. Charles's own inter-est extended from great men o'war, huge carved and gilded floating fortresses, to swift, trim yachts, the secrets of whose construction had been won from the Dutch. The king's own yacht is amongst the many beautiful vessels of the day recorded by the great maritime artists, the Van de Veldes, father and son, who had been given a studio in the Queen's House at Greenwich.

For all Charles's strong, sensuous responses to beauty, he was ultimately more of a connoisseur of all good things than a serious collector. As a man of great style he was perhaps more pre-occupied with surface than with depth and his legacy remains an evanescent one compounded of wit and laughter. The mock epitaph composed for the king's amusement by his scurrilous courtier, Lord Rochester, in its irony catches exactly his character:

Here lies a great and mighty king,
  Whose promise none relies on;
He never said a foolish thing,
  Nor ever did a wise one.

18TH CENTURY

THE AGE OF TASTE

'Après nous le déluge...'
Madame de Pompadour.

AUGUSTUS THE STRONG

Cynics said of Augustus, Elector of Saxony and King of Poland, that he was born a Lutheran, was Catholic in his ambitions, but in his private life had the habits of a Mohammedan. Augustus, as a younger brother, had never expected to succeed to the Electorate of his native Saxony, much less to wear the troubled crown of Poland. He had been able as a young man not only to commit indiscretions on a scale appropriate to his princely status, but also to travel widely throughout Europe and to indulge in all the sensuous pleasures that art, music and women could offer him.

Upon the unlooked-for death in 1694 of his brother, Johann Georg IV, Augustus found himself master of one of the richest and most civilised of the German principalities. Saxony had been in the forefront of that great spirit of reconstruction that had marked the last quarter of the seventeenth century, following the horrors of the Thirty Years War. Augustus's inheritance conditioned his whole career as a ruler, patron and collector. It embraced one of the most celebrated of the old-fashioned, heterogeneous collections of treasures, art and curiosities formed by his forebears in the sixteenth century. In addition there was the magnificent new palace in the Grosser Garten in Dresden, begun in the 1670s - the first major princely residence in the new international Baroque style in the German lands.

All this was not enough for Augustus, a man with an almost boundless appetite for luxury. In 1697 his election as King of Poland put the vast resources of a rich agricultural economy in harness with the traditional Saxon interest in technological development, thereby making possible an unparalleled expansion of Saxony's industrial base. This new prosperity enabled Augustus to embark upon lavish schemes of building and the continual enrichment of the royal collections by a stream of exquisite purchases and costly commissions.

Augustus, himself an excellent amateur architect, set out to transform Dresden from its late sixteenth-century appearance into a grand, modern capital. His ambition, as a royal builder, to reconstruct entirely the old Schloss, the Elbe wing of which which had burned down in 1701, was never to be fully realised: yet what he did achieve is perhaps more fascinating. The

In this state portrait by Louis de Silvestre, Augustus the Strong is shown in all the pride and opulence of kingship with the ancient Polish crown at his side. Augustus was almost literally the father of his people, for he had the reputation of having sired at least three hundred children besides his legitimate offspring

Zwinger, as Augustus's great complex of Baroque buildings came to be known, was compared in his day to the vast schemes of monumental public works by the Romans. But it also owed much to the extravagant but transient pavilions and triumphal arches thrown up by the scene designers of Augustus's ebullient court pageants. Light as air and delicate as spun sugar, the Zwinger was a confection. What had been begun as an orangery grew piecemeal, over the years from 1710 to 1732, yet within an overall, grand symmetrical design by Matthäus Daniel Pöppelmann, into the perfect manifestation of Augustan self-indulgence: amphitheatre and art gallery, cabinet of curiosities, royal menagerie and harem.

One of the greatest passions of Augustus's life was porcelain. His collection of fine Chinese and Japanese pieces was unrivalled in Europe and from an early date he made grandiose plans for its display in a specially constructed showplace, an enormous pavilion called the Japanese Palace, in which the various wares would be displayed in Baroque patterns upon the walls, but arranged, too, according to an entirely modern notion of stylis-

This view across the great courtyard of the Zwinger palace, painted by the Venetian Bernardo Bellotto, shows how the sprawling wings of the buildings grew out from the original central orangery

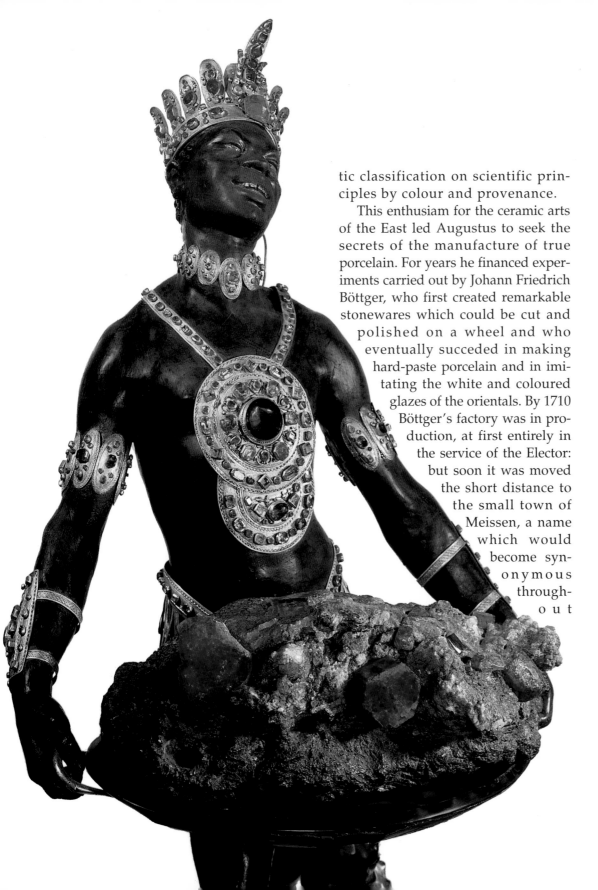

tic classification on scientific principles by colour and provenance.

This enthusiam for the ceramic arts of the East led Augustus to seek the secrets of the manufacture of true porcelain. For years he financed experiments carried out by Johann Friedrich Böttger, who first created remarkable stonewares which could be cut and polished on a wheel and who eventually succeded in making hard-paste porcelain and in imitating the white and coloured glazes of the orientals. By 1710 Böttger's factory was in production, at first entirely in the service of the Elector: but soon it was moved the short distance to the small town of Meissen, a name which would become synonymous throughout

Europe with the finest ceramic art .

Here, under the watchful eye of Augustus and encouraged by Count Brühl, chancellor of the state and a great collector and connoisseur, the factory produced an extraordinarily varied selection of wares. Tea bowls and teapots were copied from the East as were the little *blanc-de-Chine* figurines of Buddhist deities and inscrutable sages, all of which were known at this time as pagods. As more gifted artists were brought to Meissen by Brühl and the Elector, the products became increasingly sophisticated in form, technique and colouring. The incipient Rococo style makes one of its first appearances in a fanciful series of dancers, Chinamen and other exotic figurines, whilst towards the latter years of Augustus's reign the modellers of the great generation of Kirchner and Kändler were at work on a collection of life-size birds and animals, intended to embellish the interiors of the Japanese Palace.

A strain of exoticism runs through all Augustus's tastes, from his extravagant festivals and parades to his love of wild animals, which led him to finance the first zoological expedition ever sent from Europe to Africa. He inherited, too, his ancestors' passion for the intricacies of fine workmanship and delight in rare materials. It is these twin sensibilities which account for the many bizarre and wonderful objects which were made to his orders by a circle of craftsmen that included the celebrated goldsmith, Johann Melchior Dinglinger, and cunning carvers such as Balthasar Permoser. Together these two created curiosities of unrivalled quality and boundless invention, surpassing even the Mannerist treasures of the sixteenth-century Electors' fabled Secret Vault. Augustus, it seems, was an insatiable collector with wide interests. His purchases made Dresden the foremost repository of art in the German lands, for here he gathered not only the best collection of antique sculpture in the North, but also remarkable groups of ivory carvings and Renaissance and contemporary French bronzes. The traditional fields of connoiseurship such as medals he explored fully, but he broke fresh ground in the collecting of prints and drawings, gathering works by Dürer and others and significant holdings of more recent artists such as Rembrandt.

Where his ancestors had been secretive in their pride of possession,

Augustus exemplified a new attitude among princes to the importance of display. It is this ideal which, coupled with a novel conception of the intellectual value of connoisseurship and collecting as a serious scientific pursuit, led Augustus, in the 1720s and 1730s, to undertake a far-reaching and rigorous reordering of all the

Dresden collections. Everything was to be classified and the new arrangements made according to systematic principles which we can readily recognise as anticipating those of the great age of museums. Each category of the collection was rehoused in an appropriate setting: paintings in a gallery after the Italian fashion, prints and curiosities in their special cabinets and the sculptures arranged with architectural precision. The most fascinating of the treasures, including Dinglinger's masterpiece, the jewelled silver model called *The Birthday of the Great Mogul*, were placed in the Green Vaults, an Aladdin's cave of wonders, which, though formed from the strongrooms of the old castle, had in fact a door which was open to the citizens of Dresden. Though history has judged Augustus harshly, blaming him for wasting his state's riches and political power on a prodigious scale, it should be remembered that he was a cultivated and benign ruler, and among the first to be sufficiently enlightened as to grant his subjects access to the collection of which he was so proud.

Many of Augustus's greatest treasures housed in the Green Vaults were the creation of the cunning goldsmith, Dinglinger. ABOVE: A golden table centrepiece displays the finest Meissen porcelain. OPPOSITE: A carved figure of a blackamoor proffers a salver of emeralds from the Indies

LOUIS XV

The expansionist policies of Louis XIV, implemented by both military and economic means, were finally checked by the British armies led by the Duke of Marlborough, whose victories, culminating in the Battle of Blenheim, resulted in a European peace signed at Utrecht in 1713. The vaunting ambitions of the Sun King, which had carried France to a position of supreme power in Europe, were thus in his last years contained. On his death, after 72 years on the throne, he left a France secure within its own borders, peaceful and prosperous, but once again ruled by a child.

The succession had been imperilled by the untimely death of Louis's son, the Grand Dauphin, whose own eldest boy had in turn predeceased the king, leaving Louis's surviving great-grandson as his five-year-old heir. The Duc d'Orleans, the nephew of Louis XIV, and thereby cousin to the young king, was appointed as regent, and the few years of his office were chiefly remarkable for the return of the court to Paris. The reputation of this period as one of urbane sophistication and extravagant patronage derives largely from the emergence of a new class of culture-hungry bourgeois entrepreneurs, and in particular from the professional tax-collectors into whose cunning hands the State had placed the task of gathering the royal revenues.

Although the court returned to Versailles in 1722 and Orleans died soon afterwards, a new pattern of patronage of the arts and a new set of values and tastes had been established. It is perhaps significant of this new order that, as Louis XV grew to maturity, he acquired a penchant for Parisian nightlife, entering into the frivolities of his middle-class subjects and preferring the masked balls of the capital to the rarified delights of the *fête champêtre* in the park at Versailles. In this way he encountered the social group whose progressive tastes were shaping the arts in France.

For such people there was little need to cultivate the rich formality of furnishing and decoration that had prevailed under Louis XIV, and had represented the only possible style. Instead, this new class demanded light and pretty pieces of furniture, to be used informally in smaller rooms. The lines of this furniture were fluid and sinuous, deriving from shells, foliage and other natural forms. The name

*This bust of Louis XV, carved by Louis Sigisbert, casts the handsome
young king in the role of Apollo, presiding deity of the arts.
It is easy to see in this portrait the virility and wilfulness which
made him irresistably attractive to women*

*ABOVE: Louis XV was a discerning patron of the Parisian furniture-makers,
as this magnificent chest illustrates; it was made as a marriage gift to celebrate the
wedding of his heir, the Dauphin. OPPOSITE: François Boucher's Rococo
portrait of Madame de Pompadour, mistress of Louis XV, captures the aesthetic
and sensual pleasures of life at court*

Rococo, which was given first to this frilly ornament, gradually came to be applied to the fine arts and all branches of decoration.

But for the new social freedom which Louis XV had experienced as a teenager, he would never have encountered the woman who was to capture his heart and who, through her influence as the king's recognised mistress, would do so much to transform the artistic life of the nation. Jeanne-Antoinette Poisson was born into a modest but prosperous family, from which she married into the ranks of the rich, socially accepted bankers who had come to dominate finance and patronage in Paris. As Madame d'Étoiles she made a great splash in the literary salons, which were just then becoming, under the influence of philosophers and writers such as Voltaire, both intellectually significant and fashionable. But it is as the Marquise de Pompadour, the title conferred upon her by her enamoured monarch, that she is remembered to this day as one of the most influential and intelligent taste-makers in the history of royal patronage.

The king had clear ideas about architecture, but Madame de Pompadour brought a new sensibility to French decoration. She was, of course, intensely responsive to fashion, and understood how to exploit a new vogue in the most appealing and enjoyable manner. She took under her protection the painter François Boucher, who ultimately was to become the king's 'First Painter'. In Boucher's canvases we see the elegant world of the court captured with wit and charming flattery. The flickering surface of his paint is alive with the same sense of movement that in the decorative arts is associated with the Rococo. His portraits of Madame de Pompadour also display considerable insight into a woman whose power resided in her ability to amuse and hold the attention of an absolute ruler.

Louis XIV had built to express prestige and power. His successor shared these motives, of course, but the daunting scale and seriousness of architecture under Louis XIV is now modified by a grace and delicacy of detailing which marks all the finest works of Louis XV's reign. Louis's chief architect was Jacques-Ange Gabriel, who renovated the Château de Choisy for Madame de Pompadour's use, and who was employed by the king upon a succession of great public works, which were to transform Paris greatly in the years after 1752. The École Militaire was the first of these projects and was inspired by Madame de Pompadour. It was followed almost immediately by the great undertaking of laying out the Place Louis XV, known since the Revolution as the Place de la Concorde. The triumphal spaces of this great urban square are framed by two superb palaces, today the Hôtel Crillon and the Ministère de la Marine. Louis also built the new Mint, the Hôtel des Monnaies, and the Palais de Justice, both designed by Jacques-Denis Antoine.

All these projects were carried out during a time when architecture was changing very rapidly. Louis was conscious of how much the arts could do in the service of the crown. Madame de Pompadour's brother, ennobled as the Marquis de Marigny, was appointed by the king as director general of the king's building works, and in this role he encouraged numerous designers and architects who had encountered in Rome the newly fashionable ideas of the Neoclassical movement. As director general his influence was almost as great as that of his sister, though he operated through more official channels. Under Louis the director general acquired enormous and far-reaching powers to govern every aspect of public architecture

OPPOSITE: The fashion for elaborate gold boxes reached its apogee in the mid-eighteenth century. Amongst the finest of such pieces is this jewel-encrusted, double-lidded snuffbox, set with enamel portraits by Jean Ducrollay showing the king, his consort Marie Lecszinka and their children

and decoration. The centralisation that had first begun under Richelieu now became absolute, with the director general controlling the operations of the royal factories for tapestry at Gobelins, for porcelain at Sèvres and Vincennes, and the artistic programmes of the Academy and its outpost, the French School of Rome, the chief breeding ground for bright young architects and artists

Of all the royal projects none conjures up so immediate a picture of this enchantingly intelligent and enjoyable world, inhabited by the king and his mistress, as the Petit Trianon. This most elegant of tiny palaces stands in the grounds of Versailles. Gabriel began it, at the king's command, for Madame de Pompadour in 1762. She died in 1764, before she could enjoy it. Her death shattered the king, and though he went on to find solace in the arms of other and ever younger mistresses such as Louise O'Murphy, none gave him the intellectual companionship that the quick-witted Pompadour had provided. The world of the Rococo is by rights her kingdom, and she made it so the better to please her master. Though in his last decade Louis continued many of the projects he had conceived in his prime, the freshness and originality of his patronage belongs chiefly to his years with this remarkable woman.

FREDERICK THE GREAT

The creation of the state of Prussia out of the sandy and unpromising northern territories acquired by the Electors of Brandenburg in the seventeenth century was a triumph of will and statecraft for Frederick William of Hohenzollern, great-grandfather of Frederick the Great. His son Frederick, first king of Prussia, indulged himself in the building of palaces in Berlin and outside the city at Charlottenburg and Potsdam. All this magnificence was too much for his successor, who concentrated instead upon the building of a sound economy and the encouragement of modern industries. Three generations of Hohenzollerns thus established the kingdom of Prussia, in the heart of Europe, as a confident, secure and prosperous state.

Nothing in its earlier history, prior to the birth of Frederick the Great in 1712, suggested that Prussia would assume so dominant a role in the affairs of Europe as it was to do by the middle decades of the eighteenth century. It was in fact the force of Frederick's personality and the cool objectivity of his determination which made Prussia great. Bullied and berated as a weakling by his irritable and autocratic father, Frederick grew up to be a self-sufficient and ambiguous personality - on the one hand Europe's most ruthless and resourceful militarist and, on the other, a sensitive aesthete, a lover of music and a man who cared passionately about friendship.

Of his thirteen brothers and sisters, the closest to him was his sister, Wilhelmine, who was to become Margravine of Bayreuth. It was through her encouragement that Frederick took the trouble to read extensively and to study the most recent philosophical writers of the French Enlightenment. A taste for French art and literature and a talent for the flute were the last things that Frederick's father had hoped to instil in his son and heir. He sought to toughen the young prince by exiling him from court and sending him on endless military manoeuvres, from which it seems Frederick did indeed develop a penchant for war, but also one for soldiers.

In 1732 Frederick was instructed by his father to marry the Princess Elizabeth of Brunswick-Wolfenbüttel. As a married man he was allowed his own establishment and began imme-

This penetrating likeness of Frederick the Great by Anton Graff captures the unresolved conflicts in the personality of this austere but passionate man. Even out of uniform, he affected a military style

One of Frederick's most significant coups as a collector
was his acquisition of this painting of St Cecilia, the patron saint of music, by
Sir Peter Paul Rubens. Its subject must have been particularly
congenial to the soldier king for he had throughout his life
a devotion to the art of music

Frederick the Great on manoeuvres with the Prussian army.
The king's passion for all things military meant that much of his life was spent
in the field in pursuit of the glamour of conquest.
Frederick was as much loved by the common soldiers
as by his most dashing officers

diately to create for himself, at the little castle of Rheinsberg, a miniature French court. His friend and architect Georg Wenzeslaus von Knobelsdorff renovated the old schloss in an airy, Rococo style. Here Frederick could cultivate his Francophile affectations to his heart's content, correspond with the philosopher Voltaire and entertain some of the more colourful social butterflies on the European scene, such as Lord Baltimore and Count Algarotti.

The old king died in 1740 and Frederick immediately set aside his wife and his flute in order to put into action the far-reaching military campaign which he had already planned while prince. Moving swiftly against the Austrians, the Prussian army won a series of resounding victories. Frederick bemused both Maria Theresa, ruler of Austria and Hungary, and his supposed allies, the French, by negotiating with each party behind the other's back. As a result he secured the valuable territories of Upper and Lower Silesia by the Treaty of Breslau in 1742.

Having, at a stroke, made Prussia richer and more powerful than his father had ever dreamed possible, Frederick now determined to outdo his grandfather in the opulence of his patronage. The old Charlottenburg palace was redecorated on a lavish scale by Antoine Pesne, the Berlin court painter. Moreover, Frederick had in the midst of war found time to acquire the superb antiquities collection of Cardinal de Polignac. The packing cases which had arrived from Rome now yielded up their precious cargo of ancient marbles, which the king set upon the new bookcases which had been made for the royal library at Charlottenburg.

Frederick the aesthete displayed the same swiftness and resolution in connoisseurship as he had as a general in his campaigns. He knew exactly what he wanted, and when he sent Rudolf von Rothenburg to Versailles in 1744 he charged him not only with the task of worming out the King of France's secret plans, but also with a mission of artistic espionage. Rothenburg was to sniff out and acquire the best French pictures that were to be had. It was probably in this way that Frederick came to own that exquisite painting by Watteau, now known as *L'enseigne de Gersaint*, which hung in pride of place in the music room at Charlottenburg.

Even while occupied with a second Silesian war, Frederick was planning an ideal residence, smaller and more intimate than the Charlottenburg or his palace at Potsdam. He called this exquisite little pavilion Sans Souci, for he intended that his life there should be informal but graceful and without care. It was designed by Knobelsdorff to stand on a hillside of terraces, all of which were glassed in to enable Frederick to grow the soft fruits which he loved. The dining room was based on the Pantheon at Rome, while the music room was decorated by Pesne. Every evening after supper there were concerts, at which the king often played the flute. Here Frederick felt he had created the sophistication and elegance of French court life, though he himself must have been an incongruous figure, since he always dressed in uniform and military topboots.

Perhaps his fondness for military dress was a wise precaution, since war seemed to dog his footsteps. From 1748 to 1756 Frederick was allowed to enjoy his military prizes without challenge, but the Treaty of Versailles brought against him the formidable alliance of Louis XV and Maria

OPPOSITE: *Frederick's enchanting coffee house in the form of a Chinese pavilion still stands in the grounds of Sans Souci at Potsdam. It is enriched by extraordinary, life-size gilded figures of Chinamen*

Theresa, both spoiling for revenge. The ensuing Seven Years War devastated central Europe, and brought Frederick close not only to losing the territories he had so wilfully seized, but to seeing Prussia laid waste and partitioned among his enemies. Even in the depths of adversity his nerves and his taste held good. He found time in Saxony to order a service of Meissen china to be sent to one of his oldest friends in Berlin.

When, in 1763, the exhausted protagonists agreed a mutually acceptable peace, Frederick turned to less confrontational policies, consolidating his lands within the boundaries of Prussia and Silesia, and working, like his father, to create stable economic growth. In 1763 the first porcelain from the newly established Berlin works, founded and fostered by the proud king, appeared on the market. This fac-

tory, and the building, in 1763-9, of the Neues Palais at Potsdam, were the chief new artistic projects of Frederick's later years. But neither ever meant as much to him as Sans Souci. There the off-duty soldier and monarch could go over to the enemy and pretend to be a Frenchman himself, reading only French books, making music and cultivating his gardens and his friendships.

CATHERINE THE GREAT

The vast and barbarous tracts of land that were Russia had until the late seventeenth century barely been touched by the artistic and cultural fashions of western Europe. Embassies between London and Moscow had been chiefly concerned with trade. It was only with the visit of Peter the Great to the courts of Louis XIV and Charles II that the grafting of modish western trappings on to the vital but savage traditions of the old Muscovite state became the Tsar's ideal.

The great monument to Peter's determination to modernise his nation was the city of St Petersburg, which he raised from 1703 onwards upon an unpromising marshy site near the medieval port on the White Sea at Archangel. This new gateway to the West was still being built when Peter died in 1725, and of his successors none seems to have had either the time or the inclination to continue and realise his dream of a sophisticated and elegant city that would be the Paris of the Far North. It was ironic therefore that it was to be not a Romanov of the true imperial line but a young German princess who would consummate that union of the East and the West.

Catherine had been brought to Russia in 1744 as the child bride of the Grand Duke Peter, naïve son of the autocratic Empress Elizabeth. As she was later to write in her own epitaph 'at the age of fourteen she made a triple vow: to please her husband, Elizabeth and the Russian Nation.' An astute young woman, Catherine rapidly developed a political grasp far beyond that of her husband, and whilst she was disliked and humiliated by her mother-in-law she gained the trust and admiration of many at court. And so when in 1763, only a year after his accession as Peter III, the new Tsar was deposed, it was to his consort, Catherine, that the imperial throne was given.

Eighteen lonely years of marriage to an idiot whom she hated had thrown Catherine back upon her own intellectual resources. Her two chosen masters, in statecraft and philosophy, were Peter the Great and Voltaire, and she consumed avidly the writings of these two very different mentors. From the one she derived her conception of absolute autocracy imposed by a will of

The indomitable Catherine the Great painted by Giovanni Battista Lampi. She came to Russia a naïve German princess but transformed herself, through sheer force of will, into a leading patron of the arts and a ruthlessly effective autocrat

Of the several palaces which Catherine improved and beautified,
Tsarsköe Selöe remains one of the most elegant. It was remodelled by the Scottish architect,
Charles Cameron, who created the Green Dining Room (ABOVE: TOP)
and the Blue Drawing Room (ABOVE: BOTTOM).
OPPOSITE: A portrait bust of the empress by the Russian sculptor, Shubin

*A plate from the 'Frog Service' which Catherine commissioned from
the foremost English potter, Josiah Wedgwood.
The service is decorated with topographical views of English gardens
including this view of Mount Edgcumbe in Devon*

steel; from the other she developed an insatiable yearning for the intellectual brilliance of contemporary French salon society.

Catherine's patronage of the arts was intended to give visible form to both these ideals. Early in her reign she determined to establish her standing in Europe as a connoisseur and intellectual through the acquisition of major paintings and a great library. She snatched from under the nose of Frederick the Great over two hundred paintings that he had hoped to purchase for Sans Souci from the dealer Gotkowski. Similarly, when it became known that the vast collection of books and manuscripts assembled by Denis Diderot, editor of the great eighteenth-century French encyclopedia, were to be sold, Catherine's agents were instructed to bid whatever was neccessary for the entire collection.

The empress secured both Diderot's library and his own manuscripts, a prize for which she was happy to pay him a lump sum equivalent to a salary for fifty years. In doing so she also bought a golden reputation as a literary patron and the loyal support of Diderot and his friends in her pursuit of other treasures. The sculptor Falconet was recommended to Catherine by Diderot to execute a giant statue of her hero, Peter the Great, for St Petersburg. He arrived in Russia in 1766 and for many years was to act as the imperial art advisor. He, together with Galitzin, Russian ambassador to Paris, and Diderot himself, engineered over the next decade some of the most breathtaking coups in the history of collecting. Whole galleries of masterpieces, such as those formed by the Duc de Choiseul and the connoisseur Pierre Crozat, were bought *en bloc* and transported by sea to the great new museum-palace of the Little Hermitage being built by the French architect, Vallin de la Mothe.

Behind the cool, classical façades of the Hermitage Catherine was assembling at astonishing speed one of the most remarkable art collections ever seen. From Dresden had come the pictures of Count Brühl, including superb works by Rubens, Rembrandt and Ruisdael. Also from Brühl came important contemporary works by Watteau and the Italian view-painter Bellotto, who had worked in Dresden for Augustus the Strong. The Crozat collection enriched the Hermitage at a stroke with a dozen works by Rubens, seven Van Dycks, and eight more Rembrandts, as well as masterpieces by Raphael, Giorgione, and Veronese. These, together with the acquisition of several more, smaller groups of choice things, established the empress as the proprietor of a major treasure house and a fearsome Amazon in the battlefields of Europe's art trade.

In 1774 the Scottish architect Charles Cameron arrived in Russia, bringing with him the exciting new ideas of the European Neoclassicists who sought to recreate the splendours of Rome in magnificent buildings for the modern world. Catherine had summoned him, having seen his folio volume, *The Baths of the Romans*; from this she concluded that Cameron was the man to carry out the schemes that she planned to beautify the country palace at Tsarsköe Selöe. From this he went on to become her favourite architect, perhaps because the austere grandeur and scale of his work reflect precisely the empress's conception of truly imperial architecture.

Catherine's prodigality as a patron became legendary. From England she ordered the greatest service of china ever made by Josiah Wedgwood; all London came to gawp when this so-called 'Frog Service' was exhibited before it was shipped. The British were even more astonished, and connoisseurs were outraged, when in 1778 Catherine bought outright the celebrated picture collection that had been formed by Sir Robert Walpole at Houghton Hall in Norfolk. This was as great a triumph for the acquisitive autocrat as the purchase of the Crozat gallery had been.

The empress started a fashion for art and collecting and created for the first time among her nobles a real taste for European luxury in furnishing and decoration. She attracted to Russia several important French and German cabinetmakers, who taught and encouraged native craftsmen. These men in turn interpreted the classical French forms with a fundamentally Russian delight in rare materials and opulent finishes. A strange tradition also grew up of making Neoclassically-inspired furniture including chairs and desks in steel. This formal elegance barely restrains a savage, almost oriental exuberance: such cultural tensions are typical of the achievements of Catherine's reign. For all her strength of character and restless energy Catherine, like Peter the Great before her, discovered that though she might import the sophistication of France to the Russian steppes, it could never ultimately be more than an exquisite but fragile veneer.

GUSTAV III

One image perhaps conjures more readily than any other the world into which Gustav was born in 1746 and in which his remarkable sensibilities were to be formed. In 1763 the king, Adolf Frederik, prepared for his German wife, Louisa Ulrike, an enchanting surprise: on a little hill in the grounds of the royal palace at Drottningholm he set up a tiny chinoiserie pavilion which he had ordered to be made in secret in Stockholm. This present was given to the queen to mark her name day: and when she was brought to the door of the Chinese pavilion her seven-year-old son, the future Gustav III, was waiting, dressed in the costume of a mandarin, to greet her in verse and present her with the key to her new toy.

The Swedish court had since the seventeenth century been mad about all things French. From as early as 1662 Count Tessin the Elder had been at work creating, both in Stockholm and at Drottningholm, an hour's journey from the city, great royal palaces in the international Baroque style. Drottningholm was by the 1690s the Swedish Versailles. In 1744, when Gustav's parents were married and settled at Drottningholm, the young German princess placed her mark upon the palace by adding to it new suites of rooms in the lighter and more feminine taste of the Louis XV period. These she filled with fashionable French Rococo works of art and a glittering circle of Francophile Swedish intellectuals. But Gustav's

mother's greatest passion was for French theatre and Italian opera, an inheritance that would determine the life of her cultivated son and, by a strange twist of fate, bring about his untimely end.

As a youth Gustav was inevitably seduced by the glamour of the French companies who performed for his mother at the court theatre at Drottningholm. In 1766, following a fire, the architect, Karl Frederik Adelcrantz, at the queen's orders, rebuilt the old theatre in a restrained but pretty classical style. From that time Gustav became more and more involved in the staging of productions, and three years after his accession in 1774 he finally took complete control of the running of the theatre. Thereafter Gustav

Gustav III appears here with all the intuitive theatricality
of his flamboyant personality. The king's love of dressing up manifests itself
in his exotic tunic and boots, which are curiously at odds with the
elegant classicism of his surroundings

maintained the theatre and its performers entirely out of his own pocket, becoming, as it were, a royal theatrical impresario.

The theatre itself was equipped to the highest professional standards and with the latest stage machinery, which enabled the sets to be changed in a matter of seconds and thereby permitted the most sophisticated productions to be presented. Gustav's mother had favoured French plays, but her son hoped to create a new Swedish national drama. He also had a great love of opera, in particular for the newly fashionable, classical works of Gluck and his followers, which Gustav staged in Swedish. He even wrote a text himself which became the basis of one of the most important of all Swedish operas, the historical music-drama, *Gustav Wasa.*

Life at court in the summer revolved entirely around the theatre. The king supervised every aspect of its running, from checking the musical scores to choosing the wallpapers in the actors' dressing rooms. His courtiers formed a permanent cap-

Gustav's coronation was conducted with lavish production values, as this magical painting of the scene conveys

tive audience and everyone from the greatest officer of state to the humblest valet had a seat assigned to them. Fancy dress, however, was not confined to the stage. Gustav lived his life in a ceaseless round of masquerades and *fêtes champêtres* in the royal parks, for which the court were obliged appear in costume. Even on a day-to-day basis the king imposed a rigid dress code, stipulating formal dress for the palace during bad weather and an elegant informality for sunny days spent at the new Chinese pavilion. Confusion reigned, for only the king's word decided the regime for the day. This was posted on a card in the audience chamber, but since Gustav was quite capable of changing his mind several times in the course of a morning, costume changes often had to be as rapid as in the theatre.

It was not only theatre that flourished at Gustav's court. A golden age of fine and decorative art had been ushered in by the patronage of Gustav's parents, and this continued under their son. In fact the Gustavian era in Swedish art and design is as refined and elegant a period as its counterpart in England, the reign of George III. Gustav had grown up in a Baroque palace, decorated in the Rococo style. As a young man he saw the rise of the new Neoclassicism in Sweden, where some of the earliest experiments with that style, outside France, took place. By the time he was king this style dominated European

The costume which Gustav wore to the masked ball at which he was assasinated

architecture, and he immediately commanded the decoration of two small palaces, Haga Slott for himself, and Tullgarn, which he gave to his younger brother Duke Frederik Adolf, in this rich and dignified style.

One of the chief exponents of Neoclassicism in the North was the Swedish sculptor Johan Tobias Sergel, who returned to Stockholm in 1779 after several years spent absorbing the beauties of ancient Rome. Sergel was summoned home beacause it was felt that his talents were needed in the service of the king. His most important commission at this time was the heroic statue of Gustav which stands in Stockholm on the Skeppsbro. However, his most significant role in

Gustav's service was as guide or cicerone, when the king decided in 1783 to see for himself the art of the ancients in Italy. It says much for Gustav's artistic enthusiasm and independence of mind that he made this trip, for royal journeys were in those days almost unknown, unless made in pursuit of dynastic or martial aims.

On their return from Rome Gustav embarked upon new schemes of classical building and decoration with even greater enthusiasm. At the palace in Stockholm he installed a gallery, purpose-built to show off the collection of classical statuary which he had acquired on his travels. In 1791 he commissioned from the French scene designer and architect, Louis Jean Desprez, a handsome foyer to his beloved theatre at Drottningholm. Around this room stood ancient statues of Endymion and a group of eight of the nine muses.

However, he had barely six months in which to enjoy this splendid assembly room. On 16 March, 1792, a masquerade ball was planned at the theatre. As usual, Gustav threw himself into the party with gusto, moving among his court magnificently costumed in a Venetian mask and domino. The sinister anonymity of the masked revellers provided fatally easy cover for a political fanatic, and the king was shot point-blank before his guards could save him. He lingered for two weeks while the final scenes of his theatrical life were played out, and then the curtain fell.

*A scene of lavish pageantry, THE FEAST OF DIANA,
painted by Hillestrom; one of the many elaborate entertainments staged
at Drottningholm by Gustav. The king took the leading
role in these performances, while courtiers were pressed into
service as unwilling extras*

LOUIS XVI & MARIE ANTOINETTE

It is an unfairness of history for Louis XVI and Marie Antoinette that their horrific end, on the guillotine at the hands of the Parisian mob, has all but obscured any true picture of their characters and achievements. In the popular imagination, at least, that one swish of the Revolutionary blade which cut short Louis's unfortunate life has come to stand as the potent symbol of the extinction of the cultivated but corrupt, aristocratic civilisation of France's *ancien régime* by the people's ideals of *Liberté, Egalité* and *Fraternité*. It is ironic that the queen is remembered most frequently for the apparent callousness of her remark, when told that the people lacked bread, 'Let them eat cake', whilst Louis XVI has achieved immortality only by giving his name to a furniture style, rather than for any personal qualities.

One might well argue that it was not Louis's fault that he had inherited a rigid system of government. By the 1770s the rapid advance in Europe and North America of ideals of political enlightenment made this royal autocracy seem impossibly archaic. By a quirk of fate, Louis XVI stood at only one remove in the succession of French monarchs from his great ancestor, Louis XIV, a man of the seventeenth century, six generations removed from the young king. But while the world had moved on, France had stood still.

The court had been locked into the ancient rituals of daily life at Versailles for so many decades that even its oldest inhabitants could no longer remember any other way of life. These aristocrats were entirely out of touch with the grim realities of life in the French countryside, largely because, unlike their English counterparts, they never visted their estates. Similarly, no one at court understood the first thing about the practicalities of employment, industry or finance, because no one ever worked. The court was not only effete and ineffectual, but intellectually bankrupt. It is doubtful if the king recognized any of this, and those among his advisors, such as Necker and Calonne, who did, were obstructed at every turn by the ranks of the privileged, who behaved like wilful and selfish children.

Perhaps the great flowering of fine and decorative arts which occurred during Louis XVI's reign was actually

Louis XVI, by François Antoine. The grand tradition of autocracy, initiated by Louis XIV and maintained by Louis XV, reaches its fatal climax in the weak but stubborn king whose life ended upon the guillotine

ABOVE: *A romanticised nineteenth-century print of Marie Antoinette's toy farm, the Hameau, in the park at Versailles. Here the Queen played at milkmaids, while in Paris the mob was turning sour.*
OPPOSITE: *The 'Austrian Bitch', as she was called by her political enemies, here portrayed in enjoyment of her extravagance by her friend and favourite artist, Madame Vigée-Lebrun*

The Library of Louis XVI, at Versailles.
This room was created in 1774 by Gabriel and
exemplifies the elegant classical lines
of the style which bears the monarch's name

a symptom of this lax and self-indulgent aristocratic life style. Certainly many at Versailles cared more for gossip than they did for political intelligence, more for news of the latest developments in fashion or furnishings than in agriculture.

Louis, it has been held, was not lacking in private virtues but, coupled with perhaps a certain dullness, his qualities of loyalty and transparent honesty made him curiously unfitted for statecraft. In addition he had a fatal inability to make up his mind and relied too heavily upon the queen's judgement. She was the daughter of Maria Theresa of Austria, and even as a young bride in a foreign land she had been ready to show her mettle. Though vulgarly called the 'Austrian Bitch' and hated as the symbol of an unpopular alliance, she became the power behind the throne.

At the centre of this frivolous court, the king and queen cultivated a *douceur de vivre* very far removed from the brutal lives of toil conducted just beyond their gates. Within their great fantasy world, the park of Versailles, the queen played the milkmaid with tiny milkpails of the finest Sèvres china at her toy farm, while the king toyed with the costly fittings of his library desk for want of any serious employment of state or capacity for intellectual pursuits.

The library which was created for Louis upon his accession in 1774 by Jacques-Ange Gabriel, architect of the Petit Trianon, expresses the innate dignity and sobriety of the Neoclassical style. Louis XVI in fact inherited this architectural and decorative manner, for it had been introduced into France during the period of Madame de Pompadour's influence over Louis XV. However, many of the finest interiors in the new taste at Versailles were, like the king's library, created in the 1770s, when rooms such as the Garde-robe, the Grand Salon and the enchanting Salon de la Méridienne, were redecorated for the new king and queen.

At this time too the grounds of Versailles, whose enamelled parterres and bosky groves might have been painted by the brush of Boucher or Hubert Robert, were scattered with new and pretty garden buildings. The Belvedere, a fantastical rock pavilion, was decorated by Richier and Lagrenée. The queen's architect, Richard Mique, put up in 1778 the Temple of Love, whilst in 1783 he began the almost legendary Petit Hameau, a group of rustic style playhouses in which Marie Antoinette played at shepherdesses with all the authenticity of a Sèvres figurine.

Throughout their reign Louis and Marie Antoinette evinced a clear liking for the charming informality of these garden pavilions, and for the elegant sophistication of the Petit Trianon, in preference to the ponderous grandeur of the palace. The queen made few changes to the architecture of the Trianon, but filled it with the works of the finest furniture makers, such as Jacob-Desmalter, set against extravagant striped and floral silks in delicate feminine colours. Here the queen could retreat with a few intimates, such as the portrait painter Madame Vigée-Lebrun, and prattle happily over the teacups. Indeed, it was in the Petit Trianon that reality finally broke in on the queen's dream world - with the news of the mob's advance upon the gates of Versailles.

With the forcible removal to imprisonment at the Concièrgerie in Paris of the king and queen, and their subsequent murder in 1793 by the leaders of the Revolution, Versailles ceased to be the seat and symbol of French monarchy. The palace which had been erected in the great days of Louis XIV as a manifestation of power had come to represent all that was profligate and weak in his descendants.

19th CENTURY

THE AGE OF OPULENCE

'Everyone likes flattery, and when you come to royalty
you should lay it on with a trowel'

Benjamin Disraeli, remark made to Matthew Arnold

NAPOLEON I

Most dynasties are founded by an initial act of political or military opportunism. This is true of the Tudors, the Romanovs, and the Bourbons. The legitimacy or otherwise of Napoleon's claim to imperial status must always be weighed in the scales of history against the authenticity of other royal houses, which were also founded by men of superior political cunning or martial might.

When Napoleon set out upon his great Egyptian campaign in 1798 it was ostensibly to establish the power of France's Revolutionary government, the Directoire, in the Middle East, and so to challenge British commercial power in India. In fact, General Bonaparte had already conceived those personal ambitions that would carry him upon a wave of popular support to his proclamation as Emperor of the French. The Egyptian expedition was, for Napoleon, a consummate exercise in public relations. It afforded him the opportunity to create a cult of personality, based upon his self-image as a modern Alexander. Before the Pyramids he exhorted his troops by saying 'Forty centuries look down upon you', whilst at Jaffa he touched the sores of plague victims in a conscious assumption of the mythical curative attributes of a divinely appointed monarch. Bonaparte had taken with him to Egypt antiquarian scholars and artists, including Baron Vivant Denon, to examine the fragments of the great civilisation of the Pharoahs and to record his creation on its ruins of a new imperium.

Napoleon's triumphal return to Paris in 1799 was strategically timed: the Republic was threatened by foreign powers and the austere young general seemed to offer the salvation of the Revolutionary ideals. At this moment Napoleon was still the lean, campaign-toughened soldier portrayed in 1797, after his Italian victories, by the greatest painter of the radical Neoclassical school, Jacques-Louis David. It was no wonder, therefore, that the *coup d'état* by which Napoleon assumed supreme executive power as First Consul was a wild popular success. In the wake of his supposed Egyptian triumphs, Pharoahs, crocodiles and obelisks became all the rage, decorating everything from bookcases to parasol handles.

Up to this point Napoleon had had

*The imperial repertoire of Ancient Rome was called into play by the designers
Percier and Fontaine in the creation of a new style of presentation for the self-proclaimed
emperor. Gerard depicts Napoleon in coronation robes holding an eagle-capped
sceptre and wearing the laurel crown of the new empire*

very little time or money to devote to the arts. He was not unaware, however, of the important role that they could play in confirming the status of a world leader and asserting the supremacy of a new regime. He cultivated the friendship of David, who came to play an increasingly important role in the direction of the arts under Napoleon. It is David's great sequence of iconic portraits that summarize most compellingly the progress of Napoleon's career.

David's unfinished head-and-shoulders sketch made rapidly from life immediately upon the general's return from Italy captures the man of action. The great formal equestrian portrait which followed it, of Napoleon crossing the Alps, elevates the soldier to the status of hero. Quite different in mood is the great state history-painting of the imperial coronation in which Napoleon, having crowned himself, places the tiara upon the bowed head of his consort, Josephine. Perhaps the most telling image, and certainly that which pleased the emperor most, is the late portrait of 1812 in which David shows Napoleon in his study as the world-weary head of state, standing by his desk which is strewn with papers over which the candles have burnt low.

Of it Napoleon said: 'You have found me out, my dear David; at night I work for my subjects' happiness, and by day I work for their glory'.

In the early years of his power Napoleon kept David close by him. It was to David that he turned when he wanted his battles immortalised; and when David commended the work of his pupil, Baron Gros, a stream of commissions followed, as Gros recorded in minute detail each successive victory. Together they walked the streets of Paris at dawn, devising schemes for the aggrandizement of the capital. It was David, too, who introduced to Napoleon the architectural partners who would come to dominate so much of his patronage, both for great public works and in his private and domestic schemes. Pierre-François-Léonard Fontaine and Charles Percier are the great creators of the Empire style, that brash expression of modern military energy in the opulent forms of the arts of ancient Rome.

At the château of Malmaison, which Napoleon had acquired in 1799, Percier and Fontaine transformed a modest country house into a home fit for heroes. The council chamber is draped like the tent of a Roman general, and painted with trophies of helmets and

Jacques Louis David, the greatest painter of the Revolution, was chosen by Napoleon to record his coronation in the cathedral of Notre Dame in 1804. Here David represents the moment at which Napoleon, having already crowned himself, places the empress's diadem upon Josephine's head

weapons. The pretty feminine touches thought appropriate for the apartments of the wife of the First Consul are in the most graceful antique manner. Napoleon took a close interest in the work at Malmaison and devised the decorative progamme for his own workroom, the library.

When Napoleon declared himself emperor, Percier and Fontaine excelled themselves, tranforming the streets of Paris into a flagged and garlanded ceremonial route. The cathedral of Notre Dame was entirely hung with painted canvases, like the film set for some extraordinary epic. All of the works conceived by Percier and Fontaine for the emperor were imbued with this sense of epic scale and grandeur. After Josephine had fallen from favour, having failed to produce an heir, Napoleon married Marie Louise, daughter of the Emperor of Austria. She presented him with the son he so longed for, to secure his dream of a Bonaparte dynasty. For this baby, called the King of Rome, Percier and Fontaine contrived the most fantastical of cradles surmounted by an imperial eagle. They also sketched a plan for an enormous palace, which would have stood overlooking the Seine. But this project, like many others, remained no more than a dream.

In reality Napoleon had to be content with remodelling and refurbishing the existing royal palaces and cas-

tles. He imposed upon them the high Empire style which he loved, sweeping away the delicate sprigged silks of Marie Antoinette and substituting Lyons silk hangings in vibrant colours, woven in gold thread with stars, medallions, and his personal motif of a bee. In particular he left his mark upon the Tuileries, which served as his Paris headquarters, and on Fontainebleau and Compiègne, where he liked to pass the few hours of leisure that he permitted himself in the midst of affairs of state.

Napoleon's attempt to dominate

the world led him into the most megalomaniac schemes to unite beneath the roof of the Louvre as many of the world's greatest paintings and sculptures as he could obtain. As the boundaries of his empire rolled inexorably across Europe, so, behind them, carts rolled towards Paris laden with the plunder of great collections. At the height of Napoleon's triumphs, Denon, appointed first director of the new national museum in the old royal palace, found himself the curator of the greatest concentration of world-famous masterpieces ever brought together in the history of Europe.

This cultural domination was as shortlived as Napoleon's military supremacy. From the moment in 1812 when, in attempting to subjugate Russia, he overreached himself, his days were numbered. He had for more than fifteen years been the bogeyman of Europe. Now those rulers who had feared him united to defeat the French military machine. Bonaparte's humiliation at Waterloo was total, and his exile to the island of St Helena marked the absolute end of his career.

The flowering of his empire had been very brief. The plundered treasures were returned to their proper homes, and only the decoration of Percier and Fontaine and the paintings of David remained to bear witness to this extraordinary interlude.

Above: The Library at Malmaison, decorated by Percier and Fontaine; the emperor's favourite room in which he spent long hours over his papers. Opposite: Napoleon as the hero of modern times is shown in this portrait by David upon a fiery charger, crossing the Alps at the commencement of his successful Italian campaign

GEORGE IV

George III of England, known affectionately as 'Farmer George', was as his nickname suggests a down-to-earth man who liked and understood the art of other plain Englishmen, such as Thomas Gainsborough. His eldest son George, Prince of Wales, was, in contrast, quintessentially a man of fashion, a hedonist and a rake, whose palate rapidly became jaded by art and architecture, so that he was forever in search of new sensations. Some argued that it was his heir's giddy lifestyle and extravagance that drove the old king mad. Certainly the prince was, like many Princes of Wales, impatient of his father's discipline, and chafed at the financial restraints placed upon him by an ever-watchful king and Parliament.

When, in 1783, George came of age, he was at last allowed an independent establishment at Carlton House. His father's worst fears were very quickly realised, for the prince quickly became the centre of an alternative court, composed of fashionable young radical aristocrats, men of letters and dissolute wits. He also tore down the old royal residence at Carlton House, and thumbed his nose at his father's Establishment taste by choosing as architect Henry Holland, whose consummate taste had already dazzled Whig society when he designed Brooks's Club, in St James's, home of smart radicalism.

Carlton House was at once the most elegant and extravagant town palace yet seen in London. At first, French decorators, under the direction of the prince's agent, Daguerre, were imported to complement Holland's architecture and to give the state-rooms a gloss of international chic. Later, in the 1790s, 'Prinny', as he was dubbed by his circle, tired of the austere grandeur of his home and began to explore the delights of the exotic Chinese taste in decoration. The drawing room at Carlton House was decked out with elaborate draperies, hung from pagoda-roof pelmets and ornamented with tiny bells, oriental porcelain and fake bamboo.

Meanwhile, the prince had taken a mistress and decided to install her in the newly developing seaside resort at Brighton in Sussex. He rented a marine villa and immediately called in Holland to aggrandize it. But Holland's plain classical bays palled once Carlton House had been enriched

'The First Gentleman of Europe', as George IV was known, is shown here
in later life in a portrait by Sir Thomas Lawrence. The corseted but still stylish figure
of the king is clothed in austere but elegant tailoring of the kind which
he had done so much to make fashionable

The sumptuous colour plates of Pyne's ROYAL RESIDENCES capture precisely the overblown opulence of the late phase of decoration at the Royal Pavilion. Here the Music Room, in which the King himself would on occasion oblige his courtiers to listen to his singing, is seen festively lit for a great reception

with gilded dragons, and so Prince George determined to transform this discreet love nest into the stateliest pleasure dome in Europe, and himself into the master of his seraglio.

John Nash, who now entered the prince's service, was the ideal architect for this wayward patron. His imagination was fertile, his builders worked at double speed, and, most important of all, he understood his employer's particular brand of flamboyance and could translate his fantasies into slender pinnacles and plump onion domes. Inside the growing Pavilion, the Crace family firm of decorators worked with equal skill to conjure a lavish vision of the Orient. The Pavilion rapidly made Brighton into the most fashionable resort. Dandies, guards officers and the upwardly mobile crowded the fashionable promenades along the Steyne, parting discreetly as 'The First Gentleman of Europe' took the air.

Old King George, increasingly out of touch with reality, sat at Windsor,

*The true temple of hospitality at the Brighton Pavilion, the Dining Room
in which the king's celebrated chefs astonished polite society with the fecundity of their
imaginations. The table groaned with magnificent silver-gilt plate by Paul Storr,
the great Regency goldsmith*

while his errant son set the pace for high life in the capital. It was clear that the king could not rule, but Parliament was loath to place the reins of power in George's soft white hands. However, by 1811 the king's madness made a regency inescapable, and so Prinny became the Prince Regent and thus gave a name to the age.

London society was at its most glittering, for this was the era of Beau Brummell, dandy of dandies, Lord Byron, most profligate of poets, and Thomas Lawrence, prince of painters. Brummell was arbiter of style to a whole generation of Englishmen, and particularly to the prince himself, who was dazzled by the Beau's wit and

ruled by his sartorial pronouncements. Byron was Virgil to the Prince's Augustus, in this modern Rome beside the Thames: his stinging social criticism in verse finding its counterpart in the vitriolic caricature prints of James Gillray. But Lawrence, the greatest portrait painter since Van Dyck, held the mirror up to the age. It was he who fixed for all time the glamorous image of Regency society, and created the most memorable likenesses of its leader, the Prince Regent.

This hectic brilliance may in part have been a reaction to Britain's being at war with Napoleon throughout these years. It is extraordinary that at the very same time the prince was plotting with Nash the most grandiose scheme of urban development since Wren's plans for London had been abandoned. Their conception was nothing less than a grand triumphal way leading from the gates of Carlton House northwards, cutting the great crescent of Regent Street to meet the southern tip of the newly planted Regent's Park. Here, framed by Nash's long stuccoed terraces, the prince projected a summer palace. In the event the plans for the new palace came to nothing, for George III died in 1820 and his heir mounted the throne as George IV. He now had a surfeit of palaces to play with, and, wilful as ever, he destroyed the toy of his youth, the lovely Carlton House, in order to fund and furnish the as yet modest Buckingham House. In so doing he established the British royal family in the palace which has ever since then been the monarch's principal residence. Nash aggrandized the simple

seventeenth-century building, pouring over it a coating of creamy golden stone, throwing out wings, and transforming the interiors into a lavish statement of grandeur in the international palace style.

George's coronation was delayed until 1821, by which time he was playing with yet another new fashion. Turning the pages of his history book the new king hit upon the idea of staging the ceremonies, which took place at Westminster Abbey, in the Tudor style. In the event this romantic conceit resulted in some bizarre costumes for the protagonists, including velvet doublets, tights, and a rich array of feathered bonnets, which doubtless drew protests from the twelve heavily-built prizefighters who formed the king's redoubtable bodyguard.

The same strain of Gothick Revivalism coloured the king's last great project, the virtual rebuilding of Windsor Castle by the architect Jeffry Wyatville. Are as of the ancient castle untouched since medieval times and many of the rooms fitted out by Charles II's architects were recast in a distinctive modern gothic manner. Here, in spanking new baronial apartments, the increasingly stout and world-weary voluptuary waited, in his corsets, for the party to end.

George, as Prince of Wales, first held court in the lavish little palace of Carlton House. The elegant Neoclassical architecture created for the prince by the architect Henry Holland was stylish but relatively austere. Later the furnishing of the principal rooms became ever more magnificent

VICTORIA & ALBERT

The quiet domestic world in which the Duke of Kent, youngest brother of George IV, and his wife had raised their only child, Princess Victoria, could not have been further removed from the glittering indulgence and loose morals of Prinny's court. Her simple upbringing, in which the virtues of the family and the comforts of the hearth played so conspicuous a part, can hardly have prepared her for the role of queen and empress, still less for the obligations of artistic patronage.

Victoria was born into the last generation of European royalty whose status was unassailable and for whom patronage remained one of the essential obligations of monarchy. But it is fair to say that without the loving support and influence of her husband,

Prince Albert of Saxe-Coburg-Gotha, she would never have ventured upon so complete a reform of English taste as had come about by the end of the nineteenth century.

It was evident from the time of her accession in 1837 that the young queen must be matched with a suitable spouse. The obvious choice was her German cousin and the young couple were fortunate, for unlike many royal marriages, theirs, celebrated in 1840, proved a love match. Albert found his new wife demure, pretty and sensible, while for Victoria, swept off her feet from the start by Albert's virile charm and dashing good looks, a new world of European intellectual and artistic sophistication was unlocked.

Albert brought with him from Germany the newly fashionable

enthusiasm for the work of the earlier Italian painters. As a collector he had a great passion for early Renaissance panel paintings, but his real interests lay in the encouragement of new art in which he found similar virtues. There had grown up in Germany in the previous twenty years a new school of artists who, travelling to Rome for their studies, had rediscovered the qualities of quaintness and earnestness in these early masters. The Nazarenes, as they called themselves, revived the ancient techniques of fresco painting and longed for the opportunity to carry out major schemes of public art. In some German states, such as Bavaria, great works were in hand, and Albert was clearly determined that England should occupy a central place in this great revival.

'The home life of our own dear queen' was recorded in intimate detail
by the romantic brush of Sir Edwin Landseer, who delighted in portraying
the wildlife which the Prince Consort had slaughtered with
Teutonic enthusiasm and thoroughness

In 1855 Victoria and Albert were thrilled
to discover at the Royal Academy
Summer Exhibition a young English artist
who had learned his craft in the rigorous
art schools of Germany. Frederic Leighton's
painting of CIMABUE'S MADONNA CARRIED
THROUGH THE STREETS OF FLORENCE
is filled with a romantic enthusiasm for the
world of the early Italian painters.
The queen bought the picture as a present
for her beloved consort, who was forming
one of the first collections of pictures by
these artists of the Quattrocento

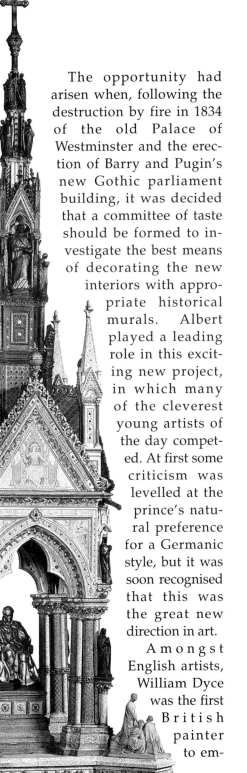

The opportunity had arisen when, following the destruction by fire in 1834 of the old Palace of Westminster and the erection of Barry and Pugin's new Gothic parliament building, it was decided that a committee of taste should be formed to investigate the best means of decorating the new interiors with appropriate historical murals. Albert played a leading role in this exciting new project, in which many of the cleverest young artists of the day competed. At first some criticism was levelled at the prince's natural preference for a Germanic style, but it was soon recognised that this was the great new direction in art.

Amongst English artists, William Dyce was the first British painter to em-

ulate the crisp draughtsmanship and philosophical austerity of the Nazarenes. The queen and Prince Albert held him in high regard and bought a number of his works. By contrast, the lush nudes of William Etty, whom Albert also admired, have a more direct appeal to the senses. Both these artists represented differing facets of what we now perceive as the Victorian sensibility. But it is the animal pictures of Edwin Landseer, with their bravura handling and sentimental themes, which seem the most expressive of the ideals of that complex age.

Landseer's popular family group, *Windsor Castle in Modern Times*, is the quintessential image of royal domestic bliss. It captures perfectly the genuine warmth of the family circle and the new intimacy that Victoria and Albert contrived to establish at each of the residences which they used at various times of the year. The queen had, of course, inherited a number of alternative official residences. Buckingham Palace and Windsor Castle were comprehensively refurbished, the former being transformed from Nash's Regency palace into a sober barracks, reminiscent of a very large commercial hotel. It was for the new family houses, at Osborne on the Isle of Wight and Balmoral in the Scottish Highlands, that Victoria reserved her affection and her best efforts at home making.

Osborne represents an early Victorian ideal of stylish elegance in the Italianate manner. There she and

Albert created a villa far from the cares of state, where their growing family might romp at will. Balmoral initiated a new fashion in Scottish baronial architecture; indeed, the royal couple's summer holiday there each year achieved the miracle of making tartan chic. Scottish houses, Scottish decoration and, in Landseer's famous painting the *Monarch of the Glen*, Scottish sports, became all the rage. The queen even penned a runaway bestseller of Scottish life, *Leaves from the Journal of Our Life in the Highlands*.

Prince Albert's energy and sense of public duty led him to take on many new responsibilities. His greatest achievement in cultural terms was the conception, with Henry Cole, of a great exhibition in which the art and industry of all the civilised world should be spread before the British public, to amaze and delight, but principally to educate and improve them. The exhibition was housed in the most remarkable purpose-built exhibition hall ever created, Joseph Paxton's Crystal Palace. The impetus which this extravaganza gave to British decorative arts was extraordinary. The Prince Consort's patronage did not, however, end with the show of 1851. His clever entrepreneurial mind had already devised a use for the profits of the exhibition. With Cole as his right-hand man, he secured the land south of Hyde Park for future exhibitions, and to establish a complex of museums, artistic and educational institutions, so creating in bourgeois South

*ABOVE: The Durbar Room at Osborne House on the Isle of Wight,
a monument to the Queen-Empress's dominion over the subcontinent of India.
OPPOSITE: The original model for the Albert Memorial, made in 1863 to
designs by Sir George Gilbert Scott*

Kensington a new cultural quarter.

In 1861, at the tragically early age of 42, Albert died of typhoid fever, in the midst of planning another international exhibition to rival that of 1851. The nation mourned, but Victoria was devastated. All her energies were reserved now for schemes which would commemorate in an appropriately elevated manner the life and achievements of her beloved consort. Sir George Gilbert Scott designed at her command the great gilded tabernacle that is the Albert Memorial, whilst all over Britain loyal subjects raised similar architectural marks of respect. Opposite the Memorial she built a vast domed concert hall, which was named the Royal Albert Hall; it stands at the high point of Albert's cultural Acropolis. Having thus manifested her grief, the queen retired into virtual seclusion at Windsor, abandoning all temporal pleasures.

NAPOLEON III & EUGÉNIE

With the untimely death in 1832 of Napoleon's only son, the King of Rome, the mantle of the Bonapartist cause fell upon the rounded bourgeois shoulders of the emperor's nephew, Louis Napoleon. He was the son of Louis Bonaparte, whom the emperor had installed as King of Holland, and Princesse Hortense Beauharnais, herself the daughter of Josephine and thus the emperor's stepdaughter.

Nature can seldom have equipped anyone so badly for the role of charismatic leader: Louis Napoleon was short, plump and had the unctuous aspect of a devious French provincial shopkeeper. But what he lacked in romantic stature he made up for in political cunning, and the single-minded determination with which he pursued the restoration of the Bonaparte dynasty. In 1836 and again in 1840 he had led unsuccessful attempts to overthrow the 'July Monarchy' of Louis Philippe. Then in 1848, the 'Year of Revolutions' throughout Europe, the house of Orleans was turned off the French throne. A new republic was declared, the second such in the history of France. So great was the power of the name Napoleon with its associations of stable government and military glory, that Louis Napoleon was elected president of the Second Republic.

The new president had inherited from his uncle a strain of ruthless tenacity. He was determined from the first to discard the masquerade of democracy when the moment was ripe. On the 2 December 1851 he engineered a *coup d'état*, assuming absolute authority: exactly a year later his status as autocrat of France was fully recognised when he became the Emperor Napoleon III.

The restoration of imperial France called for a revival of the great traditions of artistic and architectural patronage which had been established under the First Empire. Napoleon III was perfectly happy to employ the skills of those artists and architects who had been working under the old Orleans regime. To record the new imperial house he recalled to Paris François Xavier Winterhalter, the German portrait painter who had recorded the likenesses of Louis-Philippe's courtiers. In 1853 the emperor took as his wife Eugénie de Montijo, a Spanish countess and a buxom southern beauty, whose ful-

*Napoleon III painted by Hippolyte Flandrin in
conscious homage to David's great portrait of his uncle, the first Napoleon.
The furnishing and decoration in this picture make deliberate reference
to the splendours of the First Empire*

some charms were painted again and again by the facile brush of the German flatterer. The coarse-grained graces of Winterhalter's portraits reflect exactly the flashy opulence of this *arriviste* court. Perhaps the most evocative image of all is that of the empress surrounded by a bevy of her ladies-in-waiting, awash with silks and ruffles in a Watteauesque glade.

At the château of Compiègne to the north of Paris, Napoleon and Eugénie sought to create a salon. Winterhalter was the first of many painters, sculptors and men of letters to be summoned to dance artistic attendance upon the imperial couple.

These week-long parties devoted to culture, called the *Séries Elégantes*, must have been pretentious affairs, larded with ceremonial and sycophancy, but not perhaps without their amusing moments. One such is recorded when Prosper Merimée, author of the novel upon which Bizet was to base his popular Spanish opera, *Carmen*, devised a literary game of dictation. Intended for the amusement of the Empress, it badly misfired on the embarrassed writer when it revealed all too cruelly the limitations of the Spanish Eugénie's command of the French language; she made a record sixty-two mistakes.

Eugénie, who loved to dress up in the style of Marie Antoinette, was as isolated and prejudiced as her ill-fated predecessor. Her extravagance and her meddling in politics would together fatally weaken her husband's regime. One of her greatest areas of expenditure was the lavish restoration work which she initiated in the old royal palaces. The imperial court resided in Paris at the Tuileries, which became a hated symbol of Second Empire indulgence. But the empress also ordered costly renovations at Compiègne and other houses. In addition, her fantasies of past glory led her to deck out the Petit Trianon as a shrine to the life and tastes of Marie Antoinette, whilst at Malmaison she set in train a long campaign of restoration and new decoration as an act of dynastic piety.

So although Napoleon III was popular in the provinces it was almost inevitable that smart Parisians would dislike and distrust him. It has always been said that fear of a return to the pattern of revolution on the streets of the capital motivated the emperor's vast schemes of urban regeneration. When the emperor appointed Baron Haussmann to sweep away much that remained of the ancient, narrow streets of medieval Paris, he certainly had it in

The Empress Eugénie Surrounded by the Ladies of her Court,
painted by François Xavier Winterhalter, the quintessence of the Second Empire.
The luxury and frivolity of this world were immortalised
by Verdi in his opera La Traviata

ABOVE: The Imperial Foyer of the new Parisian Opera House built by Garnier, the epitome of Second Empire opulence.
RIGHT: Jean Leon Gérôme's painting of the Emperor and Empress receiving Oriental ambassadors at Fontainebleau

mind that the new wide boulevards would be less easy to barricade and would facilitate the rapid movement of troops to maintain order. Yet Haussmann not only gave the emperor security against insurrection, he also created the model for great modern cities that would be followed throughout Europe. Haussmann's

vision was conceived on the grandest scale, with long vistas each terminated by a great landmark such as the Arc de Triomphe or a major public building.

The most magnificent of these, and the great showcase of the Second Empire style in architecture and decoration, is the new opera house begun in 1861 to designs by

Charles Garnier. This was the beloved project of Napoleon and Eugénie. When the empress first saw the designs she asked the architect in what style they were conceived, since she could not recognise in them the lines of the architecture of the great eras of Louis XIV, XV or XVI. Garnier delighted her by his

courtier's reply, that this was the style of the Second Empire, the *style Napoléon Trois*.

The profligacy of the court made the regime increasingly unpopular at home, whilst the obstinacy of the emperor's foreign policy lost him allies abroad. When Bismarck, the 'Iron Chancellor' of Prussia, seeking to unite the German states, manoeuvred Napoleon into a war in 1870, France crumbled. The emperor was taken prisoner following an ignominious defeat at the battle of Sedan. Parisian democrats stormed the Tuileries, putting the palace to the torch. Eugénie, unlike Marie Antoinette, succeeded in escaping and the mob deposed the emperor and declared the rule of a Commune. Thus, though Napoleon and Eugénie were eventually reunited in exile in England, they never saw the completion of the Opéra; instead it was, by a twist of fate, destined to become the glittering symbol of the raffish elegance of France's *Belle Époque*.

LUDWIG II

The Wittelsbach family, who ruled Bavaria, had always had a penchant for building. Ludwig I, grandfather of Ludwig II, was a notable patron of the new Greek Revival style of architecture, and transformed the royal palace at Munich into a recreation of the Palazzo Pitti. His son, Maximilian II, built upon the ruins of a very ancient hilltop castle, Hohenschwangau, an idealised evocation of medieval times, in the form of a handsome Gothic fortress fitted up with elegant decorations. But for Maximilian's son building was not a hobby: it was a lifetime's obsession.

Ludwig II was a solitary child, and when, in 1864, at the age of eighteen, he became king, he was introverted, isolated from the realities of political changes in greater Germany, and from

the advance of modern technology. He had grown up at Hohenschwangau surrounded by architecture and decoration which spoke of a golden age of chivalry. This romantic past of castles and knights was more real to him than the age of the railway and the steamship. In particular his childhood home was associated in his mind with the legend of Lohengrin, the Swan Knight.

Ludwig discovered in the operas of Richard Wagner, which he studied avidly, the work of a kindred spirit. In 1861 he had seen his first production of one of these operas. This was *Lohengrin*, based upon those same chivalric tales and legends which he had loved as a boy. The effect of it upon the young and emotionally inhibited prince was overwhelming. He fell in love with the theatre: its

drama, artifice and glamour. Thenceforth his life was lived in a state of heightened theatrical emotion, and the fulfilment of his slightest wish became a subject of great moment, as though he were himself some prima donna of the stage. One of his first acts, upon becoming king, was to summon Wagner to Munich. The composer was delighted to discover in the young monarch a generous patron. So munificent was Ludwig, in fact, that after four years his ministers insisted that he banish Wagner from Bavaria, for the burden upon the national exchequer of supporting Wagner's extravagant tastes, and of staging his works in ever more lavish productions, was so great that the country was threatened with bankruptcy.

Although deprived of the company

One of the earliest in the long series of portraits commissioned by Ludwig II to bolster his romantic self-image. Ferdinand Piloty shows the king, aged nineteen, dressed in his favourite blue uniform and draped in his luxurious ermine coronation robe

ABOVE: Ludwig with his bride-to-be, Princess Sophie. Although dynastic considerations persuaded Ludwig to become engaged to his young cousin, the match never took place. The engagement was broken in mysterious circumstances, leaving the young king's reputation more compromised than before. LEFT: The Spiegelsaal at Schloss Herrenchiemsee was a deliberate attempt by Ludwig to compete with the magnificence of the Galerie des Glaces at Versailles. Louis XIV was one of Ludwig's pantheon of heroes - the ideal aesthetic autocrat

of his favourite, Ludwig was no less infatuated with the dream world of dragons and superheroes of which Wagner wrote. He seems to have adopted an entirely imaginary persona, playing out a role in which building became the substitute for heroic action. As early as 1868 he wrote to Wagner outlining his idea of a many-towered feudal castle, perched vertiginously like an eagle's eyrie upon a pinnacle of rock above his childhood home of Hohenschwangau. The castle of Neuschwanstein was conceived as an evocation in stone of the ideals and themes of Wagner's *Tannhäuser* and *Lohengrin*, its massive walls rising sheer from the rock. Yet the overall effect is curiously insubstantial, the cloud-clapped towers seeming to float in Alpine mists.

In the interiors, just as in the external detailing, Ludwig dictated to his architects and designers, Eduard Riedel, Georg Dollmann and Julius Hofmann. All three were strongly influenced by the evocative water colours which the king had commissioned from Christian Jank, who was in fact a theatrical scene-painter. The earliest rooms to be completed were all in a heavy neo-Gothic style, dark and intricate. Richly patterned textiles hang in great swags across massive doorways. The furnishings of deep brown oak, heavily carved, and intricate metalwork glint softly in the pervasive medieval gloom.

As the years progressed Ludwig's tastes moved towards a more colourful and exotic style of interior, based upon the brilliant hues and rich materials of Byzantine architecture. The throne room at Neuschwanstein is the only complete realisation of such a scheme and dazzles with its gold mosaics and serried ranks of gilded columns wrought from massive slabs of porphyry and lapis lazuli.

From the time of the Franco-Prussian war, in 1870, Ludwig withdrew increasingly even from those few duties of state in which he still showed any interest. The hideous realities of modern warfare and the cynical and devious manoeuvring of the politicians worked on his delicate sensibilities, gradually loosening his tenuous grip upon the real world. In particular he may have been perplexed by the problem of being, on the one hand, the nephew of King Wilhelm of Prussia, first kaiser of all Germany, while on the other having a strong emotional attachment to the French royal family, sharing with Louis XIV the conviction that the king is himself the state. Ludwig's absolutism largely took the form of the wilfulness of a spoilt child. He expected absolute obedience from his subjects, architects and courtiers. Any attempt to limit his expenditure met with tantrums, and the estimates prepared for his building projects acted only as challenges to greater extravagance .

In 1869 he began work on Linderhof, the second of his fantasy palaces. Where Neuschwanstein had been a feudal set piece, Linderhof was a deliberate stylistic statement of his devotion to the house of Bourbon. Ludwig took this modest wooden hunting lodge and set Georg Dollman to work coating the inside and outside in a creamy froth of Rococo ornament. The bedroom of this charming pavilion is a gilded parody of the splendours of the Sun King, complete with sweeping blue velvet baldachino and heavy gilded balustrade before the bed. From a pastel ceiling of gods and goddesses hangs a magnificent crystal chandelier. Ludwig's theatrical tastes ran to dramatic lighting effects, and in the grotto beneath Linderhof he created perhaps his greatest *coup de théâtre*. This massive artificial cavern, thirty-three feet high, was lit by electricity, so that the colours of the walls could be varied from deep blue to brilliant pink. A little shell-barge floated on the water, and the king could drift through the stalagmites and stalactites while his own private *son-et-lumière* was in progress.

Ludwig's final extravagance was perhaps the logical conclusion of his obsession with Louis XIV. Nothing would do but the creation of a complete replica of Versailles. Dollmann was again given a vast budget, which was regularly exceeded. Whilst the exterior of the palace does resemble its French model, the obsessive surface ornament and extravagant gestures of the interior decoration, such as entire chimneypieces and chandeliers of Meissen porcelain, overwhelm in the way that only the fanatical historicism of the nineteenth century can. The man who could command such monuments could not, surely, be entirely sane. Indeed, in 1886 the king was officially declared insane. Mad or visionary Ludwig certainly was, but he was also a figure of high romance and human frailty.

His life ended suddenly: the day after he arrived at Schloss Berg, where he was to be incarcerated, he was found drowned, floating in the lake, with the corpse of his doctor beside him. Whether, as has often been alleged, he was murdered by a conspiracy of his enemies, or whether, for the last time, he chose to escape from harsh reality in one final gesture of flamboyant self-destruction, will remain forever the final mystery of this extraordinary human drama.

*The richly-wrought corona chandelier at Neuschwanstein is typical
of the mad medievalism which consumed Ludwig's imagination after he had encountered
the operas of Richard Wagner. The mock-heroics of the decoration of Neuschwanstein
seemed to require only some blond Siegfried to complete the effect*

NICHOLAS & ALEXANDRA

The government of Holy Mother Russia throughout the nineteenth century had been polarised between benign autocracy and well-meaning liberalism. Tsar Alexander II had transformed the Russian social system by the emancipation of the serfs in 1861. But this had done nothing to solve the knotty economic and political dilemmas that had been thrown up by the entry of this great sprawling empire into the modern world. Russia was increasingly industrialised and prosperous; and the railways had for the first time brought the far-flung provinces into close contact with those two great centres of national and intellectual life, Moscow, the traditional capital of Muscovy, and St Petersburg, the seat of the court.

When, in 1881, Alexander II was assassinated by a Polish revolutionary student in the name of the Nihilist cause, the tragedy spelt out a grim lesson for his son, Alexander III, and still more so for his grandson, the future Nicholas II. It was clear to the new tsar and his son that liberalism was synonymous with instability and that Alexander II had dangerously undermined his own position and brought disaster upon the house of Romanov.

The Romanov's attitude to the concept of ancient Russia had always been ambivalent. On the one hand their power rested traditionally upon the unification of the many Russian lands under Muscovy by Tsar Ivan, 'the Terrible'. But on the other, generations of Russian rulers had, since the days of Peter the Great, looked westward in envy and emulation of the sophistication of the courts of Europe. Nicholas II, who became tsar in 1894, brought with him to the imperial throne all the weaknesses and none of the strengths engendered by this complex inheritance. Shortly after his accession he married Princess Alexandra of Hesse-Darmstadt, a shy and deeply religious girl whose passionate adoration of her new husband led her to encourage in him a fatal belief in the God-given authority of the tsars. It was her introspection perhaps, even more than being a foreigner in a strange land, that distanced her from the court. This, allied to her hostility towards the Dowager Empress Maria Feodorovna, her mother-in-law, threw her back upon her own limited resources .

The royal couple's mutual devotion rapidly descended into a state of inten-

A poignant group photograph of the family of the last, fated tsar
of the Romanov dynasty, Nicholas II. The tsar is seen wearing traditional Russian costume,
one manifestation of his cultural programme of 'Russification'
inherited from his father Alexander III

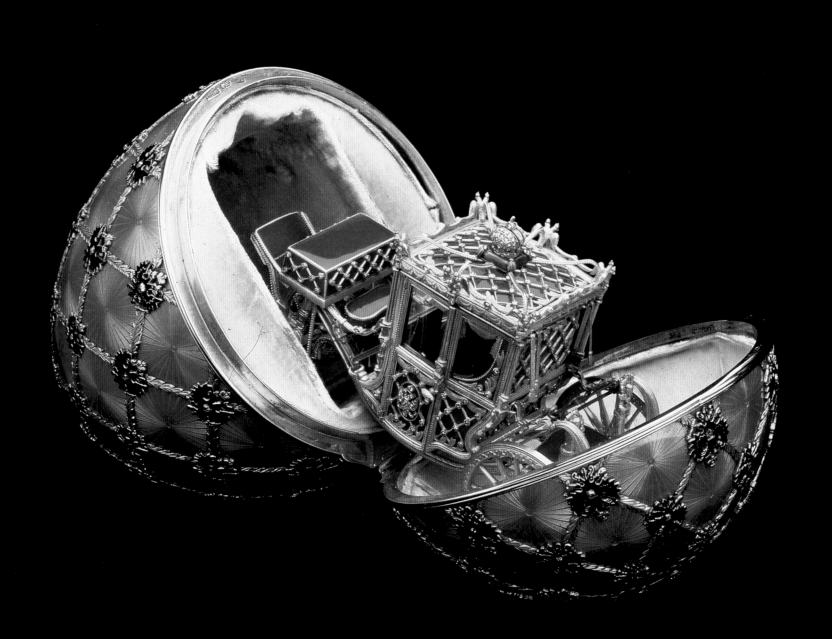

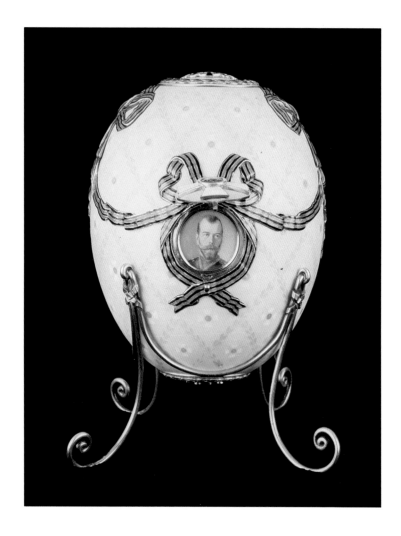

*Two of the fanciful egg-jewels created by Carl Fabergé for the traditional Easter
gift-giving between the members of the imperial family. ABOVE: 'The Cross of St George Egg'
given by the emperor to his mother in 1916, the last of these fantasies before
the revolution. OPPOSITE: 'The Coronation Egg' given by Nicholas to the tsarina in 1897
as a remembrance of their recent coronation.*

sity bordering upon the neurotic. Nicholas, egged on by the tsarina, dismissed his advisors and ruled by absolute decree, increasingly unwilling to face the calls for social and democratic reform which he regarded as 'senseless dreams'. With the birth in 1904 of the longed-for male heir to the throne, the Tsarevitch Alexis, a new intensity coloured their family life. After four healthy daughters fate had dealt them a cruel blow: the boy was discovered to suffer from haemophilia, that disease of the blood-clotting system which made every childhood scrape or tumble potentially lethal.

The tsar and tsarina followed a tradition, established in the reign of Alexander III, of giving at Easter, in Russia the most important religious festival of the calendar, Easter eggs wrought with the highest degree of sophistication by the imperial jeweller, Carl Fabergé. These legendary objects reflect all too clearly the distance between the court at St Petersburg and the lot of the common peasantry. At a time when Nihilists, Socialists and Bolsheviks were demanding a new social charter and bread for the people, Nicholas and Alexandra were absorbed in perpetuating the myth of their son's good health and demonstrating, through the sumptuous ingenuity of the mechanical eggs, an almost hysterical family loyalty.

Peter Carl Fabergé was descended from Protestants who had fled from religious persecution in France. This family of traditional craftsmen

brought with them to Russia all the intricacy and novelty of execution with which they had pleased the French aristocracy. Fabergé inherited a prosperous small business in St Petersburg from his father. His own skill lay not in making jewellery but in its design, and in the supervision of the craftsmen who actually worked the precious metals and rare stones.

Fabergé was an intelligent entrepreneur, whose cosmopolitan finesse enabled him to promote his luxury trade amongst the Russian nobility. Imperial patronage brought to him an international market, for the English royal family was as fascinated by these costly toys as were their Russian cousins. Among the remarkable keepsakes and bibelots produced are such extravagances as an egg which opens to reveal a clockwork model of the Trans-Siberian Express train, and other novelty eggs which contain complete detailed models of the Russian corona-

tion coach and the imperial yacht. Perhaps the most personal of these eggs is the Fifteenth Anniversary Egg, given by Nicholas to Alexandra in 1911 to mark their wedding anniversary.

Fabergé maintained two workshops, one in St Petersburg and another in Moscow. At St Petersburg the craftsmen worked in a more elegant western European style based, albeit distantly, upon the decorative language of the Louis XVI style. In Moscow, by contrast the Fabergé 'workmasters' were strongly influenced by the tsar's cultural programme of 'Russification'. This Nicholas had inherited from his father, whose intense conservatism led him to impress upon his diverse peoples a regime of forced assimilation. All racial groups within the Slavic patchwork of the Russian empire had been obliged to bow to traditional Muscovite culture. Nicholas took this triple crown of autocracy, orthodoxy and nationalism further, encouraging painters and craftsmen to give visual form to this ideal. Artistically the results of this revival suffered from the flaws inevitable in such propaganda. From Fabergé's Moscow workshops emerged massive, highly wrought but often ponderous figurative expressions of the spirit of old Russia. Meanwhile such painters as Repin recorded an idealised vision of Russian peasant life and scenes from ancient history which served to bolster up a largely fabricated nationalism.

ABOVE: A Fabergé frame enclosing a photograph of the young Nicholas with his cousin, later George V of England. OPPOSITE: A contemporary caricature of Rasputin manipulating the tiny, vulnerable figure of the Tsar

When the tsar and tsarina sought to hear the authentic voice of their children, the Russian people, it was the voice of the old legends and the simple life of the land that they hoped to hear. Such romantic and bogus notions presumably helped to make them susceptible to the charisma of that licentious pseudo-monk and religious charlatan, Gregori Efimovich, known to history as Rasputin. The tsarina, desperately snatching at any hope of a miraculous cure for her son's haemophilia, fell under Rasputin's spell. So malign was his influence that eventually members of the imperial family and household decided that the only possibility of salvation and sane government lay in the destruction of this false prophet.

Even the eventual assasination of Rasputin failed to restore Nicholas and Alexandra to the real world. She remained neurasthenic and obsessive, while he was absorbed in dreams of foreign conquest, pushing his country relentlessly towards war. Meanwhile, the people, starving and miserable, turned against the Little Father and Mother, booing them in the streets of the capital. Blind to the real seriousness of the situation, the Romanov dynasty plunged ever onward towards the revolutionary denouement, which commenced with the storming of the Winter Palace in 1917 and ended with the squalid tragedy of the murder of the imperial family at Ekaterinberg in 1918.

20th
CENTURY

THE AGE OF DEMOCRACY

'Democracy substitutes election by the incompetent many
for appointment by the corrupt few'

Bernard Shaw: MAN AND SUPERMAN ~ Act III

EDWARD VII

Prince Albert, the Prince Consort, brought to the education of his children the same punctilious attention to detail that characterised all his cultural and intellectual enterprises. In particular, the preparation for kingship of his eldest son, Albert Edward, was a constant preoccupation. Inevitably the solicitude of his mother, Queen Victoria, and the iron discipline imposed by his German father, backfired. Bertie became a rebel, a hedonist and a constant source of worry to his parents. His education was entrusted to a succession of tutors, each stricter than his predecessor. He was sent to university at Cambridge, the first member of the British royal family to read for a degree. The sole result was to engender in the prince a lifelong aversion to all intellectual pursuits and a fixed determination to indulge in all life's myriad pleasures.

In 1859 Bertie was packed off on an extended artistic and architectural tour in the vain hope that some European culture would rub off on him. In Paris the pedigree of the horses at Longchamp preoccupied the prince more fully than the provenance of the paintings in the Louvre. But in Rome, while visiting the studios of the international community of artists who then lived in the Eternal City, he met a young Englishman who awakened his interest in painting. Frederic Leighton was exactly the kind of artist that Bertie could understand: clever, worldly and respectful, he was also a talented painter. The prince was immediately charmed by Leighton and his work, which he knew already from the enormous picture that his mother had given to his father four years before. But Leighton was no grimly ascetic German muralist such as Prince Albert approved of. Here was a man who knew which cutlery to use, and would savour a fine cigar and an old brandy. The prince saw on the easel a canvas of a sultry Italian beauty, full of sensual promise. Immediately he offered to buy it, and though the picture was sold, Leighton, like a good courtier, immediateley offered it to the Prince, saying that he could rapidly arranged to paint a replica for the other client.

This was the beginning of a friendship which was to last until Leighton's death. When the prince and the painter next met, later that year, in London, Bertie brought the promising

In the late nineteenth and early twentieth centuries royalty and aristocracy were mad about fancy-dress balls. This portrait of Edward VII, as Prince of Wales, by Bastien-Lepage, shows him splendidly accoutred as a Venetian nobleman of the Renaissance

In collecting, as in life, Edward was a connoisseur of
fine female flesh. Frederic Leighton's portrait,
LA PAVONIA, which caught the prince's eye in Rome, is
a sensuous evocation of the luxuriant
charms of the warm south

young man into the smart and fast social set which was rapidly gathering around him. After his father's untimely death he took pains to keep his favourite artist before the notice of his mother, the queen. Thus, when the presidency of the Royal Academy fell vacant, he had brought Leighton to such social prominence that his election was almost inevitable.

Through Leighton the prince came to appreciate many of the leading French artists, whose work he saw, of course, on his increasingly frequent trips to Paris. Bastien Lepage would later paint him in magnificent Venetian fancy dress. For many years the prince was constrained in his acquisitions by his position as heir. Queen Victoria kept a firm and repressive hand upon the royal collection until her death in 1901. Meanwhile, Bertie assembled a large collection of mementoes of his good times in France, including a variety of pictures of scantily clad females, some in intricately wrought leather frames.

As Prince of Wales Bertie had something of a cult for his fun-loving great-uncle, George IV. They were alike in many ways, sharing a love of good

François Fleming's portrait of Queen Alexandra immortalises the cool Nordic grace of Edward's long-suffering queen

wine, good food and bad women, leading to a tendency to corpulence. But he also saw himself as a man of taste. On a visit to Leighton's studio he saw on the wall a print showing the rotund figure of Prinny being conducted around the Royal Academy exhibition by the then president, Sir Joshua Reynolds. 'Look, that's me with Leighton,' quipped Bertie.

When, in 1863, the prince was married to the beautiful Princess Alexandra of Denmark, he received his own establishment: Marlborough House. This gave its name to the 'Marlborough House Set', that glittering social circle of cosmopolitan aristocrats and *nouveau riche* financiers, which shaded at its periphery into a *demimonde* of gamblers, actresses and boon companions. The prince prided himself on a flair for decoration and the disposition of furniture. The reception rooms at Marlborough House were arranged with an indigestible *Belle Époque* opulence, with heavy fringed draperies, overstuffed sofas, and a profusion of potted palms and silver photograph frames. When a great ball or reception was planned the Prince and Princess of Wales would call in their friend, the president of the Royal Academy, to advise on further embellishments. The effect created by these parties was truly staggering, for in all his entertainments the prince was prodigious.

This was the era of the great country house weekend parties. Great hostesses vied to include the Waleses in their guest lists. The requisite ingredients for the success of the prince's weekends were well known: lavish food, excellent shooting, and, at the end of the day, the charms of flirtation with England's prettiest women. To ensure that his hosts understood his needs, the prince built his own house in Norfolk. Sandringham was always a home rather than a royal palace, and this long, low, redbrick seat was the ideal retreat, in which His Royal Highness could relax.

Pleasure was the prince's watchword, and his love affair with France, and, more specifically, Paris, Monte Carlo and Biarritz, led him on a series of increasingly undignified private escapades. The stories of his frolics had caused his mother much pain but this had done nothing to control his amours. During her latter days the old queen became increasingly withdrawn and Bertie took care that she should hear little of his activities. After her death, King Edward, as he now was, seemed to care little for royal propriety. He may have sealed the *entente cordiale* between the traditionally hostile French and British, but gossip attributed to him an interest in French relations far beyond the diplomatic. That luxurious life of champagne and caviar, and the perpetual scent of lavender water was doomed. The new alliance between France and Britain would very soon be tested, as the rank smell of cordite upon the fields of Flanders replaced the rich haze of Havana cigars in a war which would destroy utterly the Edwardian world.

Edward VII was introduced to the joys of motoring by Lord Montagu of Beaulieu, an early enthusiast for the horseless carriage. Here the king is seen seated beside Lord Montagu, bound like Mr Toad for the open road, in an early Daimler. It was Edward who established the royal family's loyalty to the Daimler marque

MARIE OF ROMANIA

The story of how a pretty grand-daughter of Queen Victoria was born among the Kentish apple orchards, grew up at the court of Saxe-Coburg-Gotha and found love and a great political destiny in the far-flung eastern European gypsy land of Romania is a tale worthy of Ruritanian romance. Queen Marie of Romania was not unaware of the glamour of her life. She was in many ways the first monarch to become a media celebrity. When, in 1926, she visited the United States, Americans besieged her, so great was her fame. Her autobiography, lavishly written in three fat volumes, wrings every ounce of drama from her varied exploits.

Marie's earliest years were spent in England in the typical pursuits that were thought proper, in the 1870s and 80s, for the children of the minor members of the royal family: she had an upbringing that must have differed little from that of any child of well-born parents at that date. But there was always a shadow of eagles cast even in those sunlit years, for her father, Alfred, Duke of Edinburgh, was the son of Victoria, queen and empress. Marie's early memoirs are full of the presence of the 'Mother of Europe', as the old queen was known. Through her determined pursuit of dynastic marriages Victoria had created a web of marital relationships between the royal houses of Europe, so that German, Russian and British princes and princesses were locked in a complex system of cousinage.

The Duke of Edinburgh was, by a neat family arrangement, heir to the Duke of Saxe-Coburg-Gotha, the brother of Albert, Queen Victoria's consort. Marie's family therefore went to live in that picturesque German principality. There at Schloss Rosenau life was as jolly and very nearly as English as it had been in Kent, except that more than ever Marie's days were varied by visits to Berlin or Moscow. It was on a visit to the German emperor that she met the crown prince of Romania, nephew and heir of King Carol. Love and political expediency joined hands to make an ideal match, for an alliance with a granddaughter of the queen of England as consort was exactly what the delicately balanced Romanian crown required.

Romania, by Marie's own account, was an overwhelmingly colourful kingdom, one in which peasants still

Marie of Romania seen here in 1905, when she was still
Crown Princess of Romania. Her husband succeeded to the throne in 1914,
as the old hegemony of central European royal families
collapsed before the onslaught of total war

ABOVE: The carved and guilded corner 'throne' made for Queen Marie
by three craftsmen at Castle Pelesh, the castle built by King Carol 1 at Sinaia
in the mountains of Romania. It was made in 1908, when Marie
was still Crown Princess. OPPOSITE: Carl Fabergé's replica of the crown of
Romania, made for Queen Marie as a keepsake of her royal heyday

wore the national dress, and brightened their hard lives with traditional song and dance and filled their humble homes with traditional crafts. The harsh realities of an impoverished central European kingdom were certainly very different from Marie's idealised picture, but her view of the condition of her people as happy and loyal in their grinding poverty is typical of the blinkered understanding of so many European rulers before the carnage of 1914 and the social upheavals of 1917.

The queen was, like all girls of her class, something of an artist, having learned to paint flower pictures in watercolours. But she found in the decorative traditions of eastern European art a richness which appealed to the romance of her artistic soul and spoke to her of the proud history of her adoptive nation. This seam of almost barbaric splendour was at this time enjoying a vogue throughout Europe. It was seen in the art nouveau extravagance of Budapest, the experimental art of turn-of-the-century Vienna, and coloured the pages of many art journals of the day.

Marie was eager to encourage the native crafts of Romania. She not only commissioned highly wrought pieces of furniture in a romantic and nationalistic version of the art nouveau style, but also produced her own idiosyncratic designs for such useful domestic pieces as a throne, audience chairs and a handy cabinet in which to store the crown jewels of Romania. Dressed in far from simple peasant garb, she cultivated an aura of central European fairytale mystique.

Her finest hour came in 1914. The death of the old king brought her husband Ferdinand to the throne. Where King Carol had been set upon war on the German side, his nephew maintained an uneasy neutrality. Not so Queen Marie, whose passionate identification with her adoptive people led her to recognize their longing for war with Austria, then the oppressive ruler of many Romanians dwelling in Hungary. Romania was finally tipped into the melting pot of war in 1916, struggling for survival against the forces of the Austro-Hungarian Empire and the might of Germany.

The trauma of this must have been very great, for the German royal family were Marie's cousins. Yet her own British upbringing and her fierce national pride gave her strength to support her husband, the king, and to work for victory. Her efforts were tireless. She found time in the midst of crisis to make a collection of the traditional folk tales of her land, published with pictures by the celebrated book illustrator Edmund Dulac. This book, *The Stealers of Light*, was sold in aid of the Red Cross, with whom she had been active at the front. Following the Armistice in 1918, she was equally active in the negotiations to secure a just peace, for she played a significant role at Versailles, at the peace conference in the following year.

As she herself recalled in writing her memoirs many years later, this was not the end of her story, for 'it is only fairy tales that end in being "happy ever after"'. The abdication of her husband, and the subsequent coup by which he seized power back from his son, forced Marie to summon once again all those great reserves of courage and patriotism. It was no wonder that this remarkable woman gained friends and admirers around the world. One such was Samuel Hill, an American millionaire industrialist. When, in the 1920s, he began building an extraordinary museum called Maryhill in Washington state, he begged the queen to undertake the arduous journey half way across the world to perform the opening ceremony. Marie, with characteristic pluck, set off, determined to thank Hill in person for all his fund raising and generosity in the dark days of the Great War. Her five-week journey across America became a triumphant and fêted progress from city to city. Dorothy Parker, the American humourist, even immortalised her in one of her witty quatrains:

Oh, Life is a glorious cycle of song,
A medley of extemporanea,
And love is a thing that can never go wrong,
And I am Marie of Roumania.

Had she been a star of the silver screen, her welcome could hardly have been greater. Thus it was that the granddaughter of Queen Victoria and saviour of Romania became in the last decade of her eventful life an international star, in a thoroughly twentieth century style.

*Queen Marie's casket is in the form of an ancient châsse
and decorated with repoussée work in a sophisticated, artistic style based
upon traditional Romanian craft-work*

QUEEN MARY

The nature of the modern constitutional monarchy in Britain was established by Queen Victoria, whose relationship with her government and her people forged a new and altogether more serious image of the role of the royal family. The indulgences of Edward VII's reign did not in essence change the British public's perception of its rulers. The royal family had become, in the Victorian era, the model for all families and the queen herself had become an icon of protective maternal values. She ordered the lives of her offspring to the second and third generation, arranging marriages wherever possible with her European royal cousins.

Princess Mary of Teck was born into this warm all-enveloping world. Her father was a minor German princeling, Prince Francis of Teck. Her mother was the daughter of the Duke and Duchess of Cambridge. Thus Princess May, as she was affectionately known by the Victorian public, was a great-granddaughter of George III, and among her great-uncles she numbered two more kings, George IV, for whose taste and connoisseurship she always harboured a special fondness, and William IV, the sailor king, that epitome of solid Englishness.

This perfect pedigree made her, to Queen Victoria's mind, the ideal consort for the Duke of Clarence, to whom she was betrothed for a short time before his sudden death in 1892. She then acknowledged the heavy of burden of responsibility laid upon her by the old queen, by agreeing only a year later to new plans for a marriage to the duke's younger brother George, Duke of York, who became, on the accession of his father, Edward VII, in 1901, Prince of Wales. The young couple were popular, and despite crippling shyness the Princess of Wales was determined to fulfil the role assigned to her as consort of the future king of England.

Since their marriage they had lived at York House, in the midst of the complex of royal residences clustered around St James's Palace in London. In the country their home was the more informal York Cottage, on Edward VII's estate at Sandringham. In these two houses the princess began to put together the pretty objects and pieces of good furniture which she had learned to love during her childhood at Kensington Palace. In 1910 the

Queen Mary at the Antique Dealers' Fair at
Grosvenor House in 1934 brings her formidable connoisseur's eye to bear
on a pretty trinket displayed on the stand of the old-established
Kensington firm of Delomosne

death of Edward VII precipitated the new Queen Mary into full public life at the official royal residences.

As consort to King George V her duties became still more various. But the scale upon which she could now create her effects of decoration was immeasurably greater, for now she had the run of Buckingham Palace, Windsor Castle, Sandringham and Balmoral. Queen Victoria and Edward VII had been very conscious of their proprietorship of the royal collections. But neither of them had had the instinctive historical perception and connoisseur's eye for quality that marks a truly great collector. Queen Mary's ancestry and upbringing had given her the former while her enthusiasm for visiting exhibitions, museums and dealers, had given her a unique opportunity to develop the latter. She embarked immediately upon an enthusiastic bout of the grandest possible spring-cleaning.

Her passion for museum visiting had also given her a clear understanding of the context of the royal

Princess Mary of Teck as Princess of Wales. Not surprisingly for one who had lived so much at court, the young princess was much influenced in her ideas of fashion by her mother-in-law, the queen. Alexandra had particularly favoured such high chokers of pearls

George V and Queen Mary visiting the Daimler works in 1924 to inspect their new motorcar. The queen maintained the royal association with Daimler and took great pride in the several handsome, custom-built examples that she owned up until her death

DAY NURSERY

NURSERY LOBBY

QUEEN'S BATHROOM

QUEEN'S BEDROOM

QUEEN'S WARDROBE

collections. In the early 1920s she offered to return to the Royal Pavilion at Brighton a number of important pieces of the original furniture and fittings which Queen Victoria had transported to Buckingham Palace. Queen Mary's interest in the Pavilion arose in part from her deep love of the Regency period, then only just coming back into fashion after long neglect. Over a period of thirty years she played fairy godmother to the sadly neglected seaside fantasy palace that her great-uncle George had built.

The public were well aware of the queen's devotion to art and architecture. Following her noble example to the British people during the First World War it had been decided that a tribute of some kind should be made to her: a gift from a grateful nation to the indomitable spouse of their much-loved king. Edwin Lutyens, foremost architect of the day, was commissioned to design a dolls' house, to be made and fitted out with the greatest possible craftsmanship and ingenuity. Sixty artists and 150 craftsmen laboured to create this remarkable toy. While it was being made it occupied the whole of Lutyens's drawing room.

The queen was so diverted by her present that she came often to inspect its progress, asking on one occasion, when she brought the king to see it, that they be left alone together for an hour to play with it. When it was finished, in 1924, it was exhibited in aid of charity before being installed at Windsor, where it has remained an object of great curiosity ever since.

The period during which Queen Mary's was chatelaine of the royal palaces was drawing to a close when in 1935 the silver jubilee of King George's reign was celebrated, confirming the lifelong popularity of the royal couple in the hearts and minds of the British people. Her dignity in the face of the king's death in 1936, and her strength of character in the ensuing crisis precipitated by the abdication of her son, Edward VIII, the Duke of Windsor, revealed her true mettle and inner resourses.

Queen Mary's later years were spent at Marlborough House, close to York House, the scene of her early married life. Here she was able to devote much of her time to the happy pursuit of antique hunting, a form of recreation to which she brought

formidable energy and determination. She became a familiar figure, stepping from one of her elderly and highly polished Daimler motorcars to descend upon the art dealers of Bond Street and St James's. She became patron of the Antique Dealers' Fair, held annually at the Grosvenor House Hotel. At Marlborough House she created interiors redolent of that restrained but opulent British taste which guided all her collecting. She had a particular fondness for objects with royal connections, and these gave a characteristic flavour to the elegant displays of porcelain, fans and *objets de vertu*, which filled every available surface in her handsome rooms. As a lover of pretty things, she delighted as much in finding the perfect gift for her dear friends, surprising them at Christmas with aptly chosen and often precious antiques. The regard in which she was held by dealers, collectors and curators alike was recognised, following her death in 1953, by an exhibition staged the following year at the Victoria & Albert Museum, in which the range and quality of her collections was seen in full for the first time in public.

A view looking into the Queen's Dolls' House which shows several rooms including the kitchen on the lower floor and the state bedroom above. Designed by the architect Sir Edwin Lutyens, the grand model house had decorations and miniature pictures by many celebrated artists of the day and a library of tiny books by authors such as Galsworthy, Kipling and Arnold Bennett

EDWARD VIII

The question of what style was appropriate for a modern prince was much debated in England in the early decades of the twentieth century. Queen Victoria had set a new, almost bourgeois model for the British monarchy, and although her son had rebelled against those domestic constraints, George V and Queen Mary had developed a variation on Victoria's pattern of rule, which served well until the end of the First World War. But all the certainties of society were questioned in the wake of that cataclysm. The world was changing, and the royal family was inevitably changing with it.

Edward, Prince of Wales, known to close friends and family as David, had been born a Victorian and grew up an Edwardian, but as a Georgian of the new era was able to challenge the assumptions commonly held by the Establishment about his duties and privileges. The hectic and hedonistic social whirl into which Europe plunged following the signing of the Treaty of Versailles was a clear reaction to the grim years of the Great War. The relief of those lucky enough to have survived the trenches was palpable in the air of postwar London. Meanwhile, that generation which had escaped involvement fell upon life's every pleasure with an almost guilty greed. The 'Bright Young Things' as these children of the Armistice became known, drove fast, partied hard and broke nearly all the Ten Commandments.

Life at court was staid, and the young Prince of Wales, who had a wild and rebellious streak, soon discovered the delights of café society and the fast set, of which he rapidly became the principal ornament. Like many other heirs to the throne, he was allowed his salad days. The slim, slight figure, crowned with a sleek head of golden hair, was to be seen in all the smartest places. He was perfectly in tune with the new atmosphere of informality which characterised the interwar years. He drank cocktails with the rich and famous, dined in fashionable, bohemian restaurants, and went on afterwards to dance until dawn in the new, chic nightclubs of the West End, such as The Embassy.

From his early teens he had been a 'sharp' dresser, cutting a self-consciously elegant, indeed dandified figure. With the true dandy's under-

A breezy, sporty likeness of Edward VIII as Prince of Wales
by Sir William Orpen. The prince, dressed here for golf in a knitted jumper,
plus fours and argyle stockings, made sportswear widely socially
acceptable and even fashionable

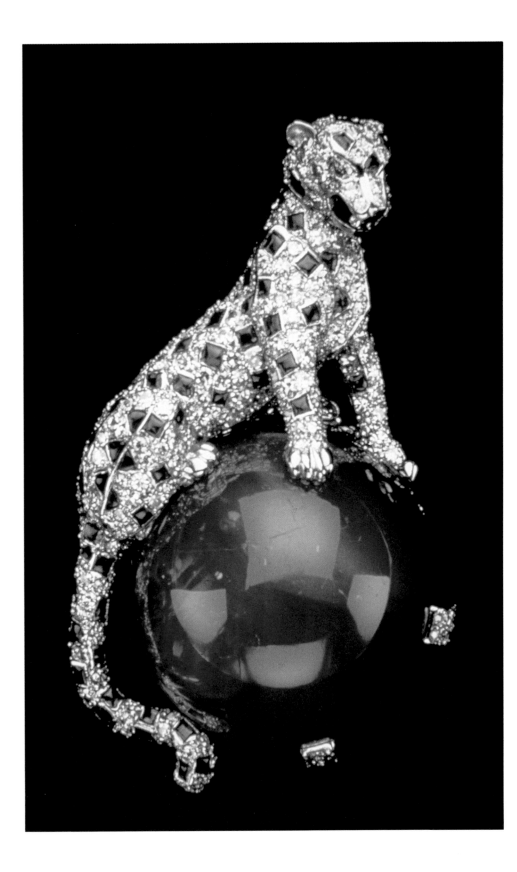

standing of dress he knew how to be innovative within tradition. He also had that instinctive feeling for the new which characterizes all trend setters. The prince favoured white waistcoats with tailcoats for formal evening dress, and his preference created the classic white-tie-and-tails image of the 1930s. At the same time, he took up the cause of the American 'tuxedo' or short dinner jacket at a time when even the middle classes wore white tie and tails for dinner and the theatre. Like the great Regency dandy, Beau Brummell, Edward became famous for the way he knotted his ties, and the geometrical precision of his 'Windsor' knots typified his dapper style.

The prince had boundless physical energy despite his small, almost fragile frame, but his position barred him from many of the natural pursuits of young Englishmen that were considered too dangerous for the heir to the throne. Instead, he threw himself into sports of every kind, in particular delighting in the fashionable games of golf and tennis and in the world of yachting. Sports clothes were just beginning to become acceptable informal wear off the court or field. The prince took up this new style with great enthusiasm.

Among the treasury of jewels which the Duke of Windsor heaped upon his wife, this Cartier brooch of diamonds and sapphires is one of the most striking

He was the first member of the royal family to be seen by his subjects in the same casual clothes that they themselves wore to relax. Vivid in jazzy argyle-knit pullovers and golfing socks, or sporting suits in the loud checks which came to be known as 'Prince of Wales', Edward took sartorial risks which only a man in his secure postion could get away with.

The prince's retreat at Fort Belvedere, near Windsor Great Park, might have been the weekend house of a fashionable London matinée idol: a place in the country, less than an hour by motorcar from the capital, with interiors so chic and pastel-hued that no muddy boot can ever have been allowed to cross the broad expanses of its pale fitted carpets. In his tastes in interiors Edward had no liking for the gilt and grandeur of the royal palaces and it is significant that he chose fashionable decorators to do up both his London residence, York House, and to modernise the Fort.

In London he had first used Hermann Schrijver, a witty socialite now better remembered, it is often said, for his dinners than his decorations. Like many of his contemporaries, Schrijver favoured long, low, comfortable sofas, convenient lamps and tables. He often arranged rooms without pictures, aiming always for a sparse, streamlined elegance that was nonetheless always underpinned by a certain feeling of unostentatious luxury. According to Schrijver, his grandest client had a distinctly modern eye,

The Duke and Duchess in later life, at their villa in the Bois de Boulogne. The Duke maintained to the end his idiosyncratic sartorial style, a blend of Savile Row and 42nd Street, while his wife emulated the contemporary chic of Jacqueline Kennedy, consort of the young president of the USA

ABOVE: The bedroom of the Duke of Windsor at his villa in the Bois de Boulogne, showing the mixture of royal objects and international decorating, which made up his personal style. The bedcover with its bold heraldic device recalls past splendours. OPPOSITE: The Windsors in their salon at the villa

preferring clean bright colours and white-painted walls: a reaction, presumably, against the formal splendours of Buckingham Palace. The greatest exponent of this style was Syrie Maugham, famous for the all white room which she had created in the house of her then husband, the writer, Somerset Maugham. That Syrie, by 1933 a divorcée, should have been not merely the prince's decorator but a favourite weekend guest at the

Fort, tells much about the new, relaxed social codes which he had encouraged.

Doubtless Syrie Maugham had found favour and patronage in the prince's circle through her close friendship with the woman who, among all his friends, was to become the catalyst for the extraordinary human drama and royal tragedy which overtook him in 1936. Syrie and Wallis Simpson were both members of that fast and hard set within which

friendship with the Prince of Wales scored the greatest possible number of social points. Less than a year after Edward had become king, the Abdication Crisis, precipitated by his infatuation with Mrs Simpson, split London society and rocked the British monarchy to its very foundations.

The king's decision to renounce the crown, a responsibility that he had come to believe he could no longer shoulder 'without the support of the

woman I love', meant inevitable exile. He travelled from London, by curious irony, in an American motorcar, a Buick. It was one more illustration of the ex-king's increasingly mid-Atlantic style. Contemporaries had remarked the curious, nasal, almost American intonation he adopted. In sartorial matters he had always affected an American bias, having his suit jackets cut in Savile Row, but ordering trousers of the same cloth from a New York tailor: an arrangement which the new Duchess of Windsor always called 'pants across the ocean'.

In exile the couple drifted in the shifting international social waters which are the usual resort of exiled monarchs and their spouses. The Duke of Windsor, deprived of his proper obligations, became painfully dependent upon his wife. The extraordinary parade of ostentatiously expensive jewels with which he showered her might almost have been a substitute for those other, royal jewels, which had so nearly been within her grasp. Cartier, Van Cleef and Arpels, and every other big name in the world of European shopping were called into service to adorn the Duchess. These treasures, and the opulent house in the Bois de Boulogne in Paris, where the Windsors ended their days, recalled the world which the Duke had sacrificed, and which he thought well lost for love.

QUEEN ELIZABETH THE QUEEN MOTHER

For all that she was born in Macbeth's castle of Glamis, Lady Elizabeth Bowes-Lyon was a thoroughly modern young woman. She grew up with the new century, and when in 1923 she married Prince George, Duke of York, younger brother of the Prince of Wales, the young couple were regarded by the British public with enormous affection. Their marriage was one more step in that democratisation of the British monarchy that had so wisely been set in train by Queen Victoria. Even in the 1920s the heir to the throne was expected to take as consort a princess of royal blood. But, with no immediate prospect of ever having to assume the great responsibility of the crown, the Duke of York had greater freedom to choose his bride for love.

The Yorks were a happy and popular couple and with the birth of their first child, the Princess Elizabeth, they presented an ideal image of British family life. In 1936 this idyll was rudely shattered by the Abdication Crisis. Suddenly the shy Duke of York, who had always been plagued by a stammer and therefore found any public duties an ordeal, found himself compelled by duty to lead his people. It was at this moment that the duchess's personal warmth and sense of style came to the fore.

The new queen was determined to make a strong and patriotic statement in her choice of a royal couturier. She turned to the young Norman Hartnell, whose work had already attracted the attention of her mother-in-law, Queen Mary. It was Hartnell who created for the young queen that look which has always remained associated with her. It is probable that Hartnell was inspired to revive the crinoline as the queen's fashion statement both by the king's suggestion that he look at the Winterhalter portraits in the royal collection, and by the succcess on the London stage, in 1937, of the popular costume-piece, *Victoria Regina*. The queen's opulent ballgowns provided a perfect foil for her English rose beauty. Furthermore, they proved a glorious backdrop to the fine Victorian settings of many of the royal jewels.

Hardly had the king and queen had a chance to set their stamp upon the new reign before they found themselves called to face an even greater test as Europe teetered uneasily on the brink of conflict. During that last

Queen Elizabeth photographed by Cecil Beaton
on the terrace of the garden front of Buckingham Palace. One of the memorable
sequence of romantic images captured in a single day's shooting,
on the eve of the Second World War

ABOVE: *Walter Sickert's* ENNUI, *one of Queen Elizabeth's fine
collection of paintings by modern British artists.*
OPPOSITE: THE ROYAL FAMILY AT BREAKFAST AT ROYAL LODGE,
WINDSOR: *an evocative conversation
piece by Sir James Gunn*

summer before war broke out the queen summoned the fashionable photographer, Cecil Beaton, to create a portfolio of royal images. These pictures of her dressed in flowing gowns by Hartnell, and shaded by a delicate parasol, are redolent of a timeless royal grace and dignity, but their significance was to lie far beyond their nostalgic charm as latter-day Winterhalter portraits. For they seemed to distill the very essence of all those things that the British held most dear and for which they would willingly sacrifice so much in the dark years ahead.

When in 1941 the full horror of total war was brought home to the British people by the aerial bombardments of the Blitz, the king and queen recognized that it was vital that they should offer personal support to those who had been made homeless in the bombing. Their visits to the East End of London marked a watershed in the relationship between the royal family and their subjects. At the same time, the threat which the Luftwaffe posed to the British architectural heritage gave the queen the inspired idea to commission from the artist John Piper a remarkable series of water colours of Windsor Castle.

These atmospheric works stem from a very British tradition of topographical painting. They are, in a quite different way, as expressive of the neo-Romantic sensibility, so closely associated with the 1930s and 1940s in England, as Beaton's photographs of the queen. The king, when he first saw the dark and brooding images of storm clouds settling over the castle battlements, remarked with a flash of the dry wit that was all his own, that it was a pity that Piper had had such bad luck with the weather!

With peace came an all too brief period of happy family life, so perfectly rendered in Sir James Gunn's modern conversation piece of the royal family at Royal Lodge, Windsor. The tragically early death of the king, in 1952, forced Queen Elizabeth to draw again upon that spirit which had enabled her to face so many challenges, and create for herself a new life and a unique role in British post-war public life.

Queen Elizabeth has always enjoyed looking at and collecting modern art. She had followed the careers of many young painters and sculptors, and now, at Clarence House, she began to bring together a distinguished and very personal choice of works of art. Her taste for such important modern masters as Piper, Henry Moore and Graham Sutherland, is complemented by her delight in such very English artists as the landscape painter, Edward Seago, who also became a good friend. Her collecting has ranged widely in modern British art, but a clear theme can be discerned. Painters in the figurative tradition, with a strong feeling for bold painterly effects, feature largely. There are works by Walter Sickert, Sir William Nicholson, Duncan Grant and Augustus John, the most colourful figure in English portraiture of the mid-twentieth century.

Her quick connoisseur's eye has also led her to pick out from dealers and auction rooms some remarkably fine and associative royal portraits. Perhaps the most interesting of these are an infinitely moving picture of Charles I at his trial, by Edward Bower, and a most glamorous Jacobite portrait of Prince Henry Benedict Stuart, by Louis-Gabriel Blanchet. Queen Elizabeth's enthusiasm for the Turf is reflected in her choice of very good horse pictures by J.F. Herring. All of these works might be characterised as the best of British taste, but with a subtle, individual twist. They provide a witty and personal counter-point to the more formal nature of the official royal collections, giving to the rooms at Clarence House the charm and easy informality that is so characteristic of Queen Elizabeth herself.

Windsor Castle, one of the series of large water colours
commissioned from John Piper by Queen Elizabeth as a gift for
King George VI. Piper's moody evocations are characteristic of the
modern romantic school of British painting
of the late 1930s and 1940s

THE PRINCE AND PRINCESS OF WALES

The Queen and the Duke of Edinburgh laid the foundation of Prince Charles's personality and pre-occupations when they decided that their eldest son should be educated, unlike any previous heir to the throne, at a conventional school. The rough and tumble of boarding school life at Gordonstoun in Scotland certainly gave the young prince a clearer insight into the pleasures and problems of life in the real world. The philosophy of Gordonstoun's founder, Kurt Hahn, which placed such emphasis upon the great outdoors, self-reliance and a strong sense of duty to the community, sowed seeds which have born fruit which would, perhaps, have surprised Hahn, who was certainly no aesthete.

Charles's first personal encounter with ceremonial came at his symbolic investiture as Prince of Wales, at Caernarvon Castle in 1969. The scene was set in an ancient Welsh stronghold and consciously evoked the barbaric splendour of the days of Edward, the Black Prince. An almost futuristic crown was placed upon the prince's head by the queen, to the accompaniment of the echo upon castle walls of a distant fanfare of trumpets.

Following school he went on to take a degree at Cambridge: another royal innovation. It was here that the prince began to show his originality and independence of character, cutting a popular and humorous figure in university theatricals. After a conventional royal stint in the services, during which Charles served, like his great-uncle Lord Mountbatten, in the Royal Navy, he was confronted, like all Princes of Wales, with the challenge of defining his role in the nation. At first he explored paths similar to those which his father had mapped out in the 'Duke of Edinburgh's Award Scheme', establishing his 'Prince's Trust' in 1977 as a personal contribution to the celebration of the silver jubilee of his mother's reign. The Trust has subsequently done much to encourage young people, with a particular emphasis upon those from poor and deprived backgrounds.

His engagement in 1981 to Lady Diana Spencer brought to the house of Windsor the glamour of a young and beautiful consort, and was greeted with rapture by the British public. The wedding in 1982 broke with royal tradition by being solemnized in St Paul's Cathedral, rather than in

Brian Organ's portrait of the Prince of Wales aroused considerable controversy when it was unveiled. The prince is shown in casual dress, seated eccentrically against a fence, above which appears his flag. It is far from a conventional state portrait but captures something of the intensity of the sitter's character

Westminster Abbey. It was the media event of the year; and the worlds of royal pageantry, high fashion, and the theatre united to make of it, as journalists delighted in pointing out, a fairy-tale event.

The new princess established herself immediately in the sartorial tradition begun by Queen Elizabeth, the Queen Mother. She adopted a striking image, contrived for her by the designers Elizabeth and David Emanuel, who had created the lavish wedding dress of ivory silk taffeta in which she had made such an impression on her wedding day. Since then she has diversified her patronage, but always within the sphere of British fashion, favouring in particular Bruce Oldfield, Catherine Walker and Victor Edelstein. Edelstein has proved to be a worthy successor to Hartnell for the present generation of young royals. It is his stylish and dramatic evening gowns that often have contributed so greatly to the Princess of Wales's sensational appearances at many galas. The prince and princess have shown themselves to be enthusiasts for both opera and ballet, lending further royal glamour to both of these art forms.

The prince proved to be an exacting patron in the ordering of a royal residence, when he and the princess acquired Highgrove House in Gloucestershire. Charles's interest in correct architectural detail and its application to modern living became one of his chief preoccupations at this time. In this we may perhaps identify the influence of his royal ancestor and hero, George III, who was himself fascinated by architecture and made detailed drawings under the tutelage of the royal architect Sir William Chambers. In the 1980s the prince entered the public arena of architectural debate, casting himself in the role of champion of traditional values and human scale in design.

At a dinner in the Fountain Court at Hampton Court Palace, before an audience of architects, he berated the profession in a deliberately polemical speech, castigating them for lack of concern both for the people who live in their creations, and for the poverty of the modern design repertoire. He took as an example of all that was, in his view, rotten in the state of architecture, Richard Rogers's newly published scheme for an extension to the National Gallery in Trafalgar Square.

This he denounced, in a memorable phrase, as 'a monstrous carbuncle on the face of an old and much-loved friend'. Press and public reaction followed immediately, with some supporting the prince for his forthright views, whilst others, chiefly architects, criticised him for daring to have an opinion at all. In fact he was simply expressing the concerns and reservations of many laymen, who had watched with increasing alarm the architectural rape of Britain since the Second World War. Not since the days of Albert, Prince Consort, had a member of the royal family proved to have such a sensitive grasp of the issues, or the energy to act effectively upon that understanding.

The prince's architectural interests have borne fruit in an influential television programme, which lucidly argued his case for a humane architecture for the late twentieth century. These ideas also formed the basis for an exhibition, and achieved more permanent form in his widely read and much discussed book, *A Vision of Britain*. He has shown himself to be equally concerned with the development of small-scale community-based building. Another manifestation of his

Painted later, after her marriage, Organ's companion piece to his portrait
of the prince shows the Princess of Wales seated similarly eccentrically, sideways on a chair.
Both pictures convey the ambivalence of the young couple
to conventional ideas of royal grandeur

beliefs is the master plan which he has commissioned from Leon Krier, the leading post-Modern architectural theorist, for a new village, to be built outside Dorchester, in Dorset, upon the prince's own lands in his domain of the Duchy of Cornwall.

He has most recently been drawn towards the ecology movement, and the 'Green Issues' as they are popularly known, contemplating and commenting upon our planet's struggle to survive. No prince in modern times has shown himself more serious or more thoughtful for the fate of his land. A recent likeness, commissioned by the prince himself from the painter, Tom Wood, whose work he had discovered in an exhibition, is no formal state portrait. Rather, it reveals a sensitive and contemplative man, a prince with an desire to see his future realm renew itself in such a way that it can face the next century with confidence.

The prince's intervention in the architectural debate surrounding the fate of Paternoster Square led him to commission an alternative scheme in his favoured classical style from the architect John Simpson, shown here in an oil painting by Carl Laubin. The modest scale and traditional detailing of this complex of offfice buildings reflects the Prince's own conviction that modern architecture must answer to human needs

BIBLIOGRAPHY

Unless otherwise stated, all books listed below
were published in London

GENERAL

Fisher, H.A.L. *A History of Europe*, 1936
Haskell, F. & Penny, N. *Taste and the Antique*, 1981
Honour, H. *Chinoiserie: The Vision of Cathay*, 1961
Impey, O. & MacGregor, A. *The Origins of Museums*, Oxford, 1985
Pope-Hennessy, J.W. *The Portrait in the Renaissance*, Princeton, NJ, 1980
Strong, Roy. *Art and Power*, 1583 *Splendour at Court*, 1974
Trevor-Roper, Hugh. *Princes and Artists*, 1976
Victoria & Albert Museum. *Princely Magnificence* (Ex. Cat.), 1980
Walpole, Horace. *A Catalogue of the Royal and Noble Authors of England*, 2 vols, 1759

16TH CENTURY

Cellini, B. (Ed. Tamasin, A.). *The Autobiography of Benvenuto Cellini*, 1969
Hachet, F. *Francis the First*, 1934
Queen's Gallery, London. *Holbein and the Court of Henry VIII*. (Ex. Cat.), 1978
Strong, Roy. *The Cult of Elizabeth*, 1977
Tuena, F.M. *Il Tesoro dei Medici*, Florence, 1988
Waas, G.E. *The Legendary Character of Maximilian*, 1941
Walsh, W.T. *Philip II*, 1938

17TH CENTURY

Erlanger, P. *Louis XIV*, 1970
Evans, R.J.W. *Rudolf II and his World*, Oxford, 1973
Fraser, Lady Antonia. *King Charles II*, 1979
MacGregor, A. *The Late King's Goods*, 1990
Magne, F. *La Vie Quotidienne au Temps de Louis XIII*, Paris, 1964
Stolpe, S. *Christina of Sweden*, 1966
Trevor-Roper, Hugh. *The Plunder of the Arts in the 17th Century*, 1970
Whinney, M. & Millar, O. *English Art, 1625-1714*, Oxford, 1957

18TH CENTURY

Carlyle, Thomas. *History of Friedrich II of Prussia*, 1899
Cronin, Vincent. *Catherine, Empress of all the Russias*, 1978 *Louis and Antoinette*, 1974
Hillestrom, H. *Drottningsholms Teatern*, Stockholm, 1956
Jones, Stephen. *The Eighteenth Century*, Cambridge, 1985
McInnes, I. *Painter, King and Pompadour*, 1965
Mitford, Nancy. *Frederick the Great*, 1970
National Gallery, Washington. *The Splendor of Dresden* (Ex. Cat.), 1978
Racinais, H. *Versailles Inconnu: les petits Appartements des Roys Louis XV et Louis XVI*, Paris, 1950
Souchal, G. *French Eighteenth-century Furniture*, 1961
Watson, F. *Louis XVI Furniture*, 1960

19TH CENTURY

Barnett, C. *Bonaparte*, 1978
Blunt, Wilfred. *The Dream King*, 1970
Darby, E. & Smith, N. *The Cult of the Prince Consort*, 1983
Longford, E. *Victoria R.I.*, 1964
National Portrait Gallery. *Franz Xavier Winterhalter* (Ex. Cat.), 1987
Priestley, J.B. *The Prince of Pleasure*, 1969
Victoria, HRH The Queen. *Leaves from a Journal of Our Life in the Highlands*, 1868
Watkin, D. *The Royal Interiors of Regency England*, 1984

20TH CENTURY

Beaton, Cecil. *Diaries, The Wandering Years: 1922-39*, 1961
Channon, Sir Henry. *Chips: The Diaries of Sir Henry Channon*, 1967
Charles, HRH The Prince of Wales, *A Vision of Britain*, 1989
Cowles, Virginia. *The Last Tsar and Tsarina*, 1977
Gernsheim, H. *Edward VII & Queen Alexandra*, 1962
Hayward Gallery. *The Twilight of the Tsars* (Ex. Cat.), 1991
Holden, Anthony. *Charles, Prince of Wales*, 1977
Longford, E. *The Queen Mother*, 1981
Marie of Romania. *The Story of My Life*, 1934-5
Pope-Hennessy, James. *Queen Mary 1867-1953*, 1959
Windsor, Duke of. *A King's Story: The Memoirs of HRH the Duke of Windsor*, 1951

INDEX

Page numbers in *italic* refer to the
illustrations and captions

Aachen, Hans von *55*
Académie Française 103
Adelcrantz, Karl Frederik 117-19
Admiralty (Britain) 89
Adolf Frederik, King of Sweden 117
Albert, Prince Consort 13, 143-7, *143-7*, 169, 171, 200
Albert Memorial, London 147, *147*
Alexander II, Tsar 161

Alexander III, Tsar 161, *161*, 164
Alexandra, Queen of England *171*, 172, *181*
Alexandra, Tsarina 161-5, *163*
Alexis, Tsarevitch 164
Algarotti, Count 108
Ammanati, Bartolomeo 44
Anne of Austria *63*, 79
Anne of Cleves 23

Antique Dealers' Fair *181*, 185
Antoine, François *123*
Antoine, Jacques-Denis 102
Arcimboldo, Giuseppe 57
Armada Jewel *36*, 38
Arthur, King of Britain 18
Arundel, Thomas Howard, Earl of 67-8, *71*
Augsburg *19, 27*

Augustus the Strong, Elector of Saxony 93-7, *93-7*, 115
Austro-Hungarian Empire 108, 178

Balmoral 13, 146, 182
Baltimore, Lord 108
Bandinelli, Baccio 44
Banqueting House, Whitehall 68-71, *68*
Baroque style 62, 82, 85, 93-6, 117, 120

Barry, Sir Charles 146
Bastien Lepage, Jules *169*, 171
Bavaria 143, 155-8
Beaton, Cecil *193*, 196
Beauharnais, Princesse Hortense 149
Bellotto, Bernardo *94*, 115
Berlin 105, 175
Berlin porcelain 109
Bernini, Giovanni Lorenzo 71, *71*
Biarritz 172
Bismarck, Prince Otto von 153
Blanchet, Louis-Gabriel 196
Blois 33
Bonaparte dynasty 149
Bosch, Hieronymus 51, *51*
Böttger, Johann Friedrich 94
Boucher, François *101*, 102, 127
Bourbon dynasty 131, 158
Bower, Edward 196
Bramante 33
Brandenburg, Electors of 105
Brighton 137-8
Brighton Pavilion 138, *138-9*, 185
Brittany, Duke of *79*
Bronzino, Agnolo 33, *42*, 44
Brooks's Club, London 137
Brosse, Salomon de 62
Brueghel, Jan 'Velvet' *57*
Brühl, Count 94, 115
Brummell, Beau 139, 188
Buckingham, George Villiers,
    Duke of 67
Buckingham Palace, London 140, 146,
    182, 185, 190, *193*
Budapest 178
Burgkmair, Hans *6*, 21, *21*
Burgundy, Duke of *79*
Burlamachi 71
Byron, Lord 139
Byzantine style 158

Cabinets of Curiosities *57*
Caernarvon Castle 199
Calonne, Charles Alexandre de 123
Cambridge, Duke and Duchess of 181
Cambridge University 169, 199
Cameron, Charles *112*, 115
Carlton House, London 137-8,
    140, *140*
Carol, King of Romania 175 , 178
Cartier *188*, 191
Castiglione, Baldassare 7-12, 29
Catherine the Great, Empress of

Russia 111-15, *111-14*
Catholic Church 26, 47-8
Cellini, Benvenuto *30*, 33, *42*, 44,
    44 , 51
Chambers, Sir William 200
Chambord 33
Champaigne, Philippe de *61*, 62
Charlemagne, Emperor 29
Charles, Prince of Wales 199-202,
    199-202
Charles I, King of England 2, 12,
    61, 67-71, *67-71*, 196
Charles II, King of England 85-9,
    85-8, 111
Charles V, Emperor 47, 55
Charles X Gustavus, King of
    Sweden 77
Charlottenburg Palace 105, 108
Chelsea Hospital, London 88, *88*
Choiseul, Duc de 115
Choisy, Château de 102
Christina, Queen of Sweden 73-7, *73-6*
Cimabue *144*
Clarence, Duke of 181
Clarence House, London 196
Clouet, Jean *29*, 33
Colbert, Jean Baptiste 86
Cole, Henry 146-7
Compiègne 134, 151
Congreve, William 88
Cornwall, Duchy of 202
Correggio 71
Cortona, Domenico da 33
Corvus, Johannes, *23*
Counter-Reformation 48, 51
Coysevox, Antoine 82
Crace family 138
Cromwell, Oliver, 2,12, 85
Crozat, Pierre 115
Crystal Palace, London 146

Daguerre (George IV's agent) 137
Daimler cars *172*, *183*
David, Jacques-Louis 131, 132,
    132, 134, *135*, *149*
De' Rossi (carver) *45*
Dee, Doctor John 57
Delomosne (antique dealer) *181*
Descartes, René *74*, 77
Desprez, Louis Jean 120
Diana, Princess of Wales 199-200, *200*
Diderot, Denis 114-15
Dinglinger, Johann Melchior 97, *97*

Directoire 131
Dollmann, Georg 158
Dolls' House, Queen Mary's 185, *185*
Dorchester 202
Drake, Sir Francis 38
Drake Jewel *36*, 38
Dresden 93-7, 115
Drottningholm 117-20, *121*
Ducrollay, Jean *102*
Dulac, Edmund 178
Dürer, Albrecht *17*, 18, 21, 59, 74, 97
Dyce, William 146

Easter eggs, Fabergé *163*, 164
École Militaire, Paris 102
Edelstein, Victor 200
Edinburgh, Alfred, Duke of 175
Edinburgh, Prince Philip, Duke of 199
Edward VII, King of England 169-72,
    169-72, 181, 182
Edward VIII, King of England 12,
    185, 187-91, *187-90*
Egypt 131
Ekaterinberg 165
Eleonora of Toledo 41, *42*, 44, 45
Elizabeth, Empress of Russia 111
Elizabeth, The Queen Mother *12*,
    193-6, *193-7*, 200
Elizabeth I, Queen of England 35-8,
    35-8
Elizabeth II, Queen of England
    193, 199
Elizabeth von Brunswick-Wolfenbüttel
    105-8
Elizabeth of York *23*
Eltham 26
Emanuel, David and Elizabeth 200
Empire style 132, 134
England: Charles I 67-71; Charles II
    85-9; Edward VII 169-72; Edward
    VIII 187-91; Elizabeth I 35-8;
    George IV 137-40; Henry VIII 23-7;
    The Prince and Princess of Wales
    199-202; Queen Elizabeth, the Queen
    Mother 193-6; Queen Mary 181-5;
    Victoria and Albert 143-7
Enlightenment 105
El Escorial 47-51
Etty, William 146
Eugénie, Empress 149-53, *151-2*
Eworth, Hans *35*, 37

Fabergé, Carl 163, 164, *165*, 176

Falck *73*
Falconet, Étienne-Maurice 115
Ferdinand I, Emperor 18
Ferdinand I, King of Romania 175, 178
Field of the Cloth of Gold *23*, 27, 33
Flandrin, Hippolyte *149*
Flemlng, François *171*
Florence 17, 41-4, *41*, 57, 62
Fontaine, Pierre-François-Léonard
    131, 132-4, *135*
Fontainebleau 32, 33, 134
Fontainebleau, School of 33
Fort Belvedere, Windsor 189, 190
Fouquet, Nicolas 79
France, 47, 117, 171, 172; François I 29-
    33; Louis XIII 61-5; Louis XIV 79-83;
    Louis XV 99-103; Louis XVI 123-7;
    Napoleon I 131-4; Napoleon III and
    Eugénie 149-53
Francis, Prince of Teck 181
François I, King of France 7, 23, 27,
    29-33, *29-32*
Frederick I, King of Prussia 105
Frederick II the Great, King of Prussia
    105-9, *105-8*, 114
Frederick William of Hohenzollern 105
Frederik Adolf, Duke 120
French Revolution 123, 127, 131
French School of Rome 103
'Frog service' (WEDGWOOD PORCELAIN)
    114, 115,

Gabriel, Jacques-Ange 102,
    103, *126*, 127
Gainsborough, Thomas 137
Galitzin (Russian ambassador) 115
Garnier, Charles 152-3, *152*
Gascoigne, George *36*
George III, King of England 120
    137, 138-9, 140, 181, 200
George IV, King of England 137-40,
    137-40, 143, 171-2, 181, 185
George V, King of England *165*, 181-2,
    183, 185, 187
George VI, King of England 193,
    196, *197*
Gerard, François-Pascal-Simon *131*
Germany,]43,]46, 178;
    Augustus the Strong 93-7;
    Frederick the Great 105-9;
    Ludwig II 155-8;
    Maximilian I 17-21;
    Rudolf II 55-9

Gérôme, Jean Leon *152*
Giambologna 44, 55, 74
Gillray, James 139
Giorgione 2, 115
Gluck, Christoph Willibald 119
Gobelins tapestries 103
Goltzius, Hendrik 59
Gonzaga family 12, 71
Gothick Revival 140
Gotkowski (dealer) 114
Grabmal 18
Graff, Anton *105*
Grand Dauphin *79*
Grant, Duncan 196
Great Exhibition (1851) 146
El Greco 51
Greek Revival 155
Greenwich 26, 27, 85-6, 89
Gros, Baron 132
Gunn, Sir James *194*, 196
Gustav III, King of Sweden 117-20, *117-21*
Gustavus Adolphus, King of Sweden 73
Gwynn, Nell *86*, 88-9

Haga Slott 120
Hahn, Kurt 199
Hampton Court Palace *26*, 200
Hapsburg dynasty 17, 41, 47, 55, 57, 59, 73
Hardouin-Mansart, Jules 82
Hartnell, Norman 193, 196, 200
Haussmann, Baron 151-2
Henri IV, King of France 61, 62, *63*, 79
Henrietta Maria, Queen 85
Henry, Prince of Wales 67
Henry VII, King of England 23, *23*
Henry VIII, King of England 7, *7*, 17, 23-7, *23-7*, 29, 33, 35
Hermitage, St Petersburg 115
Herrera, Juan de 48
Herring, J.F. 196
Highgrove House, Gloucestershire 200
Hill, Samuel 178
Hillestrom *121*
Hilliard, Nicholas 35-7, *36*, 38
Hofkirche, Innsbruck 18, *19*
Hofmann, Julius 158
Hohenschwangau 155, 157
Hohenzollern dynasty 105
Holbein, Hans 23, *23*, 26
Holland, Henry 137, *140*

Holy Roman Empire 17, 29, 55
Hôtel Crillon, Paris 102
Hôtel des Monnaies, Paris 102
Houghton Hall, Norfolk 115
Hradschin castle, Prague 57, 58
Hungary 55, 178

India 131
Innsbruck 18, *19*
Invalides, Paris 88
Isle of Wight 146
Italy 29, 33, 41-4, 47, 55, 120, 143
Ivan 'the Terrible', Tsar 38, 161

Jacob-Desmalter 127
James I, King of England 67, 68
Jank, Christian.158
Johann Georg IV, Elector of Saxony 93
John, Augustus 196
Jones, Inigo 68, 71, 85
Jonson Ben 71
Josephine, Empress 132, *132*, 134, 149

Kändler 94
Kennedy, Jacqueline *189*
Kensington Palace, London 181
Kent, Duke of 143
Killian, Lucas 59
Kirchner 94
Knobelsdorff, Georg Wenzeslaus von 108
Königsmark, Count 74, *76*
Krier, Leon 202
Kunstkammern 57

La Mothe, Vallin de 115
La Tour, Georges de 65
Lagrenée 127
Lampi, Giovanni Battista *111*
Landseer, Sir Edwin *143*, 146
Largillière, Nicolas de *79*
Lawrence, Sir Thomas *137*, 139-40
Le Brun, Charles 79, 82
Le Nôtre, André 79, 82
Le Vau, Louis 79, 82
Lecszinka, Marie *102*
Leemput, Remigius van *23*
Leighton , Frederic *144* , 169-71, *170*, 172
Lely, Sir Peter *86*, 88
Leo X, Pope 29
Leonardo da Vinci 29-33, *31*
Linderhof 158

Lohengrin 155
London 23, 26, 68-71, 86-8, 115, 139-40, 146, 187, 189, 196
Longchamp 169
Louis XIII, King of France 61-5, *61-3*, 79, *79*, 82
Louis XIV, King of France *11*, 12-13, 79-83, *79-83*, 86, 88, 99, 102, 111, 123, *157*, 158
Louis XV, King of France 99-103, *99-102*, 109, 127
Louis XVI, King of France 123-7, *123-6*
Louis Bonaparte, King of Holland 149
Louis Philippe, King of France 149
Louisa Ulrike, Queen of Sweden 117, 119
Louvre, Paris 61, 62, 134, 169
Low Countries 47
Ludwig I, King of Bavaria 155
Ludwig II, King of Bavaria *11*, 13, 155-8, *155-9*
Lully, Giovanni Battista 82
Luther, Martin 26
Lutyens, Sir Edwin 185, *185*

Machiavelli, Niccolo 7
Madrid 47-51
Malmaison, Château of 132-4, *135*, 151
Mannerism *32*, 33, *42*, 44, 48-51, 57, 74, 97
Mantegna, Andrea *68*, 71
Mantua, Dukes of 12, 71
Marck, Robert de la 29
Maria Feodorovna, Dowager Empress of Russia 161
Maria Theresa, Empress of Austria 108, 109, 127
Marie, Queen of Romania 175-8, *175-9*
Marie Antoinette, Queen of France 123-7, *124*, 134, 151
Marie Louise, Empress 134
Marigny, Marquis de 102-3
Marlborough, Duke of 99
Marlborough House, London 172, 185
Mary, Queen, 181-5, *181-5*, 187, 193
Maryhill, Washington 178
Massys, Jan 74, *76*
Matthias, Emperor 59
Maugham, Somerset 190
Maugham, Syrie 190
Maximilian I, Emperor *6*, 17-21, *17-21*, 23, 27, *27*, 59
Maximilian II, King of Bavaria 155

May, Hugh 88
Mazarin, Cardinal 77, 79
Medici, Alessandro de' 41
Medici, Cosimo de' 33, 41-4, *41-5*
Medici, Lorenzino de' 41
Medici, Marie de' 61-2, *61, 63, 65*
Medici family 57
Meissen porcelain 94, *97*, 109, 158
Merimée, Prosper 151
Michelangelo 33, *44*
Milan 29
Ministère de la Marine, Paris 102
Mique, Richard 127
Montagu, Lord *172*
Monte, Hans de 57
Monte Carlo 172
Moore, Henry 196
Moscow 161, 164, 175
Mount Edgcumbe, Devon *114*
Mountbatten, Lord 199
Munich 155

Napoleon I, Emperor 131-4, *131-5*, 140, 149, *149*
Napoleon II, King of Rome 134, 149
Napoleon III, Emperor 149-53, *149-52*
Nash, John 138, 140, 146
National Gallery, London 200
Nazarenes 143, 146
Necker, Jacques 123
Neoclassicism 102, 115, 120, 127, 131
Neuschwanstein 157-8, *159*
Newmarket 88
Nicholas II, Tsar *12*, 13, 161-5, *161-5*
Nicholson, Sir William 196
Nonesuch Palace 26-7
Notre Dame, Paris 134
Notre Dame des Victoires, Paris 62

Oldfield, Bruce 200
Organ, Brian *199*, *200*
Orleans, Duc d' 99
Orpen, Sir William *187*
Osborne House, Isle of Wight 146, *147*
Ovid 51
Oxenstierna, Count Axel 74-7

Palais de Justice, Paris 102
Palais du Luxembourg, Paris 62, *65*
Palais Royal, Paris 62
Palazzo della Signoria, Florence 41-4, *41*
Palazzo Pitti, Florence 62, 155

INDEX

Pantheon, Rome 108
Paris 62, 86, 88, 99, 102, 131, 132, 134, 151-3, 169, 172, 191
Paris Opéra 152-3, *152*
Parker, Dorothy 178
Paternoster Square, London *202*
Paxton, Joseph 146
Pepys, Samuel 89
Percier, Charles *131*, 132-4, *135*
Permoser, Balthasar 97
Pesne, Antoine 108
Peter III, Tsar 111
Peter the Great, Tsar 111, 115, 161
Petit Hameau, Versailles *124*, 127
Petit Trianon, Versailles 103, 127, 151
Petitot, Jean I *83*
Philip II, King of Spain 47-51, *47-50*
Philip IV, King of Spain 67
Piloty, Ferdinand *155*
Piper, John 196, *197*
Place de la Concorde, Paris 102
Place des Vosges, Paris 62, *63*
Place Royale, Paris *63*
Poland 93
Polignac, Cardinal de 108
Pompadour, Madame de *101*, 102, 103, 127
Pöppelmann, Matthäus Daniel 94
Porcelain: Berlin 109; Meissen 94, *97*, 109, 158; Sèvres 103, 127; Wedgwood *114*, 115
Potsdam 105, 108, *108*, 109
Poussin, Nicolas 62
Prague 55-7, *59*, 73-4, 77
Primaticcio, Francesco *32*, 33
Prince's Trust 199
Prussia *see* Germany
Pugin, A.W.N. 146
Pyne *138*

Queen's House, Greenwich 85, 89

Rameau, Jean Philippe 82
Raphael 29, 67, 115
Rasputin 165, *165*
Ravaillac, François 61
Red Cross 178
Regency period 139-40, 185
Rembrandt 97, 115
Renaissance 7-12, 17, 18, 23, 29, 55, 143
Repin, Ilya 164
Restoration 85, 88
Reynolds, Sir Joshua 172

Rheims 79
Rheinsberg 108
Richelieu, Cardinal *61*, 62, 77, 79, 103
Richier 127
Riedel, Eduard 158
Robert, Hubert 127
Rochester, Lord 89
Rococo style 94, 102, 103, 108, 117, 120, 158
Rogers, Richard 200
Roman Empire 132
Romania, 175-8
Romanov dynasty 131, 161, 165
Rome 77, 102, 108, 115, 120, 143, 169
Rose, John *85*
Rosso Fiorentino 33
Rothenburg, Rudolf von 108
Royal Academy 171, 172
Royal Albert Hall, London 147
Rubens, Sir Peter Paul *61*, 62, *65*, 67, 71, *106*, 115
Rudolf II, Emperor 55-9, *55-9*, 73-4, 76, 77
Ruisdael, Jacob van 115
Russia: Catherine the Great 111-15; Nicholas and Alexandra 161-5

Sadeler, Aegidius 59
St Albans, Duke of *86*
St Helena 134
St James's Palace, London 181
St Paul's Cathedral, London 86, *86*, 199-200
St Petersburg 111, 115, 161, 164, 165
Sandringham, Norfolk 172, 181, 182
Sans Souci 108, *108*, 109, 114
Sarajevo 13
Sarrazin, Jacques 62
Sarto, Andrea del 33
Saxe-Coburg-Gotha, Duke of 175
Saxony 93-7, 109
Schloss Berg 158
Schloss Herrenchiemsee *157*
Schloss Rosenau 175
Schrijver, Hermann 189-90
Schweinberger (GOLDSMITH) 59
Scotland 146
Scott, Sir George Gilbert 147, *147*
Seago, Edward 196
Sergel, Johan Tobias 120
Sèvres porcelain. 103, 127
Seymour, Jane *23*
Shubin *112*

Sickert, Walter *194*, 196
Sigisbert, Louis *99*
Silesia 108, 109
Silvestre, Louis de *93*
Simpson, John *202*
Sophie, Princess *157*
South Kensington 147
Spain 33, 47-51, 62
Spanish Armada 38
Spenser, Edmund 37
Spranger, Bartholomeus 57-9
Stockholm 73, 74, 117, 120
Storr, Paul *139*
Strigel, Bernhard *21*
Stuart, Prince Henry Benedict 196
Stuart, Prince James *12*
Stuart, Princess Louisa *12*
Stuart dynasty 68, 85
Sutherland, Graham 196
Sweden, 73-7, 117-20

Tessin, Count, the Elder 117
Theodoric the Ostrogoth 18
Titian 33, *47*, *48*, 51, 67, 71
Toledo, Juan Bautista de 48
Torrigiano, Pietro 23
Treviso, Girolamo de 26
Tsarsköe Selöe *112*, 115
Tudor dynasty 23, 37, 131
Tuileries, Paris 134, 151, 153
Tullgarn 120
Turks 55
Tuscany, Grand Duke of 51

United States of America 175, 178, 191

Van Cleef and Arpels 191
Van de Velde, Willem the Elder 89
Van de Velde, Willem the Younger *88*, 89
Van Dyck, Sir Anthony 67, 71, *71*, 115
Vasari, Giorgio *41*
Vatican 29
Vaux-le-Vicomte 79-82
Verdi, Giuseppe *151*
Veronese 115
Versailles *11*, 13, *80*, 82-3, 99, 103, 108, 123-7, *124*, *126*, *157*, 158
Victoria, Queen of England 13, 143-7, *143-7*, 169, 171, 175, 181, 182, 185, 187, 193
Victoria & Albert Museum,

London 185
Vienna 178
Vigée-Lebrun, Madame *124*, 127
Vincennes 103
Vischer, Peter 18
Vivant Denon, Baron 131, 134
Voltaire 102, 108, 111-14

Wagner, Richard 13, 155-7, *159*
Walker, Catherine 200
Walpole, Sir Robert 115
Watteau, Antoine 108, 115
Webb, John 85
Wedgwood, Josiah *114*, 115
Westminster, Palace of 146
Westminster Abbey, London 23, 140, 200
Whigs 137
Whitehall Banqueting House, London 68
Whitehall Palace, London 23, *23*, 26, 68
Wilhelm I, Kaiser 158
Wilhelmine, Margravine of Bayreuth 105
William IV, King of England 181
Winchester 88
Windsor, Duchess of *12*, *189*, 190-1, *190*
Windsor, Duke of *see* Edward VIII, King of England
Windsor Castle 88, 138, 140, 146, 147, 182, 185, 196, *197*
Winter Palace, St Petersburg 165
Winterhalter, François Xavier 149-51, *151*, 193, 196
Wittelsbach family 155
Wolsey, Cardinal *26*, 79
Wood, Tom 202
Wrangel, Count 74
Wren, Sir Christopher 86, *86*, 88, 140
Wyatville, Jeffry 140
Wycherley, William 88

York Cottage, Sandringham 181
York House, London 181, 185, 189

Zweibrücken, Charles Gustavus of 74
Zwinger palace, Dresden 94-6, *94*

ACKNOWLEDGEMENTS

The publishers wish to thank the following photographers and organisations for their kind permission to reproduce their photographs in this book:

Archive fur Kunst und Geschichte, Berlin 11;
Artothek 104, 107;
Bavaria Bildagentur 156, 159;
Berkeley Castle, Gloucestershire 68;
Bildarchiv Preussisches Kulturbesitz, Berlin 106;
Reproduced by permission of the Trustees of the Denys Eyre Bower Trust 87;
Bridgeman Art Library 140-1/Albertina Graphic Collection, Vienna 16/ Alte Pinakothek, Munich l00/ Château de Compiegne, France, Giraudon 150-1/ Coram Foundation 88/ Hermitage, Leningrad ll0/ Alan Jacobs Gallery 89/ Louvre, Paris, Giraudon 60/ Museo del Prado, Madrid 122/ Royal and Ancient Golf Club, St Andrews 186/ Tsarskoe Selo 112/ Château de Versailles, France 125;
Brighton Borough Council, the Royal Pavilion Art Gallery & Museum 138, 139;
British Antique Dealers Association/ Delomosne & Son Ltd 180;
Reproduced by courtesy of the Trustees of the British Museum 36, endpapers;
Camera Press Ltd/Cecil Beaton from *Royal Portraits* by Weidenfeld & Nicolson 192;

Anita Corbin & John O'Grady/ Royal Academy Magazine/ Dean of St Paul's Cathedral 86;
Crown Copyright and reproduced with the permission of the Controller of HMSO 26;
Drottningholm Nationalmuseum, Stockholm 118-9, 121;
English Heritage 147;
ET Archive 152-3, 154/ Musée Carnavelet 63/V&A 83;
Mary Evans Picture Library 12 left, 124, 164, 182;
Explorer 152/J L Bohin 80;
Forbes Magazine Collection, New York/Peter Curran 163/ Larry Stein 162, 165;
Garden Picture Library/ Ulrich Timms 109;
Giraudon/Malmaison 134;
Claus Hansman, Munich 19, 96, 97;
Kunstistorisches Museum, Vienna 18, 20, 30, 58, 59;
Leighton House Art Gallery & Museum 170;
Courtesy of Maryhill Museum of Art 174, 176/Bill Bachuber 177/ Wilma Roberts 179;
Metropolitan Museum of Art, gift of Mr & Mrs Charles Wrightsman 103;
National Motor Museum 173, 183;
National Portrait Gallery 193, 198, 201;
Reproduced by permission of the Trustees of the National Swedish Portraits Collection 76, 116;
All rights reserved copyright Museo del Prado, Madrid 46, 48-9, 50, 56-7;
Private Collection 38-9;
Reproduced by gracious permission of

Her Majesty Queen Elizabeth 8-9, 22, 24-5, 34, 69, 70, 136, 142, 144-5, 168, 171, 184;
Reproduced by gracious permission of Her Majesty Queen Elizabeth The Queen Mother 12, 194, 197;
Reunion des Musées Nationaux/ Fontainebleau 32/ Louvre 4, 31, 64, 65, 66, 132-3/ Château de Malmaison 135/ Versailles 10-11, 74-5, 80-1, 126,148;
Rex Features 13, 191;
Board of Trustees of the Royal Armouries, London 27;
Royal Armoury, Stockholm/ G Schmidt 77, 120;
Scala 40, 42, 43, 44, 45;
John Simpson & Partners 202-3;
South West Wiltshire Museum/ Brixie Jarvis Collection 114;
Staatliche Kunstsammlungen Dresden 92, 94/5;
Sunday Times Magazine/ Derry Moore 190;
By courtesy of the Board of Trustees of the Victoria & Albert Museum 48, 54, 84, 98, 113, 146;
Reproduced by permission of the Trustees, The Wallace Collection, London 78, 101;
Weimar Archive 6, 21, 72, 157, 160.

The publishers would also like to thank The Society of Authors on behalf of the Bernard Shaw Estate for kind permission to quote the extract from *Man and Superman* on page 167.